NEW DIRECTIONS FOR HIGHER EDUCATION

Martin Kramer, *University of California, Berkeley*
EDITOR-IN-CHIEF

Information Literacy: Developing Students as Independent Learners

D. W. Farmer
King's College

Terrence F. Mech
King's College

EDITORS

Number 78, Summer 1992

JOSSEY-BASS PUBLISHERS
San Francisco

INFORMATION LITERACY: DEVELOPING STUDENTS AS INDEPENDENT LEARNERS
D. W. Farmer, Terrence F. Mech (eds.)
New Directions for Higher Education, no. 78
Volume XX, number 2
Martin Kramer, Editor-in-Chief

© 1992 by Jossey-Bass Inc., Publishers. All rights reserved.

No part of this issue may be reproduced in any form—except for a brief quotation (not to exceed 500 words) in a review or professional work—without permission in writing from the publishers.

Microfilm copies of issues and articles are available in 16mm and 35mm, as well as microfiche in 105mm, through University Microfilms Inc., 300 North Zeeb Road, Ann Arbor, Michigan 48106.

LC 85-644752   ISSN 0271-0560   ISBN 1-55542-754-5

NEW DIRECTIONS FOR HIGHER EDUCATION is part of The Jossey-Bass Higher and Adult Education Series and is published quarterly by Jossey-Bass Inc., Publishers, 350 Sansome Street, San Francisco, California 94104-1310 (publication number USPS 990-880). Second-class postage paid at San Francisco, California, and at additional mailing offices. POSTMASTER: Send address changes to New Directions for Higher Education, Jossey-Bass Inc., Publishers, 350 Sansome Street, San Francisco, California 94104-1310.

SUBSCRIPTIONS for 1992 cost $45.00 for individuals and $60.00 for institutions, agencies, and libraries.

EDITORIAL CORRESPONDENCE should be sent to the Editor-in-Chief, Martin Kramer, 2807 Shasta Road, Berkeley, California 94708.

Cover photograph and random dot by Richard Blair/Color & Light © 1990.

The paper used in this journal is acid-free and meets the strictest guidelines in the United States for recycled paper (50 percent recycled waste, including 10 percent post-consumer waste). Manufactured in the United States of America.

Contents

Editors' Notes 1
D. W. Farmer, Terrence F. Mech

1. Education for the Information Age 5
Patricia Senn Breivik
To be effective in a rapidly changing environment, individuals need more than a knowledge base. They also need techniques for exploring new information, connecting to other information, synthesizing it, and utilizing it in practical ways.

2. Information Literacy and Accreditation: A Middle States Association Perspective 15
Howard L. Simmons
A regional accreditation agency promotes information literacy as an essential element in the improvement of the teaching and learning process.

3. Linking Undergraduate Education and Libraries: Minnesota's Approach 27
Linda Bunnell Jones
Resource-based learning and information literacy skills play important roles in the Minnesota State University System's efforts to improve the quality of education.

4. An Academician's Journey into Information Literacy 37
Lois M. Stanford
Faculty members' use of resource-based learning methods is frequently the result of changes in how they view their teaching.

5. Natural Partners: Resource-Based and Integrative Learning 45
John R. Porter
With resource-based learning, students develop a better sense of the information resources available, the nature of scientific literature, and the characteristics of scientific writing.

6. Teaching Resource-Based Learning and Diversity 55
Kelley Emmons McHenry, J. T. Stewart, Jennifer L. Wu
Students' enhanced information skills can be used to improve their understanding of different cultures.

7. Information Literacy and a College Library: 63
A Continuing Experiment
Judith Tierney
The integration of resource-based learning and information literacy into the curriculum of a private liberal arts college is a continuously evolving activity.

8. Information Literacy at Universities: Challenges and Solutions   73
Marvin E. Wiggins
Large universities face unique challenges in developing and sustaining information literacy programs.

9. Expository Writing and Information Literacy: A Pilot Project   83
Marianne I. Gaunt, Stan Nash
Evaluation of an information literacy program's effectiveness is important. Assessments of a pilot project to integrate information literacy into a university's undergraduate curriculum are made by students, faculty, and librarians.

10. The Electronic Library and Literacy   91
Jan Kennedy Olsen
Technological advances have changed our definitions of literacy and our ways of preparing literate individuals.

11. Information Literacy: Overcoming Barriers to Implementation   103
D. W. Farmer
Fundamental attitudinal and behavioral changes must take place before institutions can implement effective information literacy programs.

12. Transforming Campus Culture Through Resource-Based   113
Learning
James L. Pence
Support of resource-based learning requires the creation of learning communities of faculty and administrators who willingly cultivate campus cultures hospitable to information literacy.

AFTERWORD   123
D. W. Farmer, Terrence F. Mech

INDEX   127

Editors' Notes

At a time when it was theoretically possible to have all of the world's recorded knowledge stored in one room, a college graduate, as late as the early seventeenth century, needed only a working knowledge of Latin and Greek to be literate enough to read and use that recorded information. As scientific discoveries were made and new areas of knowledge created, the curricula of American colleges incorporated these advances and subsequently redefined what it meant to be educated. Today, when the sum of the world's recorded information is growing exponentially, the ability to read in any language is a necessary but insufficient standard of literacy. To be literate in an information-rich age means being able to identify what information is needed, to locate that information, to evaluate it, to synthesize it, and to apply it.

As the quality and quantity of information needed to function in our social institutions increases, colleges and universities are being asked to graduate students who are information literate and can operate independently in a rapidly changing, complex, information-rich environment. Information literacy is not something that is added to the curriculum, rather it is the result of resource-based learning found throughout the curriculum. Resource-based learning actively involves students in the complex process of recognizing the need for information, identifying and finding the relevant information, evaluating it, organizing it, and using it effectively to address problems. Lectures and predigested textbook information alone do not prepare students for life in an information-rich environment. Students must become information literate, that is active learners who can integrate the increasing number of information resources available to them.

These curriculum changes, like others before them, are needed if colleges and universities are to keep pace with the world at large. These changes will not come easily or overnight. Nor can they be brought about by only one segment of the academic community. Institutionwide commitment is needed, for there are numerous ways to facilitate and develop students' information literacy, requiring the diverse talents and expertise of a wide range of faculty and staff. However, colleges and universities making the effort to develop the information skills of their students can draw and build on the experience of each others' programs. Indeed, many existing and future information literacy programs owe an intellectual debt to earlier and ongoing efforts such as the program developed by the library and classroom faculty at Earlham College, Richmond, Indiana.

This volume, *Information Literacy: Developing Students as Independent Learners,* explores the concept of information literacy as an essential element in defining an educated person living and working in the Information

Age. The strategy to achieve this goal centers around resource-based learning, which requires students to critically analyze and synthesize information from a wide variety of sources available outside of the traditional classroom. The goal is to develop students as active learners who can obtain, integrate, and apply information from diverse sources. These learners will be empowered in today's information-rich environment. This is, in fact, a means of facilitating the longstanding liberal arts goal of preparing students for lifelong learning by enabling them to think critically.

In Chapter One, Patricia Senn Breivik explains the importance of information literacy and resource-based learning before looking at the evolution of the information literacy movement. Howard L. Simmons, in Chapter Two, provides the rationale and history of a regional accreditation body's interest in promoting information literacy as a way to improve the teaching-learning process. The Minnesota State University System's efforts to improve the quality of undergraduate education through resource-based learning and a strong emphasis on information skills are described by Linda Bunnell Jones in Chapter Three. Minnesota's framework for the academic library of the future is also presented.

The next several chapters provide a look at how classroom and library faculty are dealing with the challenge of developing students' information skills. In Chapter Four, Lois M. Stanford talks about her metamorphosis as a faculty member and her goals for advancing information literacy as an administrator. John R. Porter, in Chapter Five, tells of the efforts of biology and library faculty to form a partnership and develop assignments that require the application of information skills within the context of an undergraduate biology major. In Chapter Six, Kelley Emmons McHenry, J. T. Stewart, and Jennifer L. Wu describe how the process of enhancing students' information skills is used as a means to improve students' understandings of different cultures. Judith Tierney, in Chapter Seven, looks at an evolving information skills program and the lessons learned at King's College in Pennsylvania.

Although colleges have traditionally been active in the effort to improve students' information skills, Marvin E. Wiggins, in Chapter Eight, examines the efforts of large universities in this regard. In Chapter Nine, Marianne I. Gaunt and Stan Nash report on the developing information literacy program at Rutgers University. The electronic library and the skills required to use its resources are explained by Jan Kennedy Olsen, in Chapter Ten, as she describes Cornell University's efforts to prepare information literate graduates.

All information literacy programs have to clear a number of obstacles. D. W. Farmer, in Chapter Eleven, enumerates some of the barriers that faculty, librarians, and students must overcome if colleges and universities are to meet the challenge and improve students' information skills. In Chapter Twelve, James L. Pence calls for the substantive transformation of higher education through resource-based learning. In this new educational culture, active learners from the faculty and the administration join together to accept the challenge to create and support resource-based learning environments that facilitate students' intellectual development. In the Afterword, we close the volume by summarizing common themes that run throughout resource-based learning and information literacy efforts.

D. W. Farmer
Terrence F. Mech
Editors

D. W. FARMER *is vice president for academic affairs at King's College, Wilkes-Barre, Pennsylvania.*

TERRENCE F. MECH *is director of the library at King's College.*

People whose education consists of lectures and textbooks are not well prepared for problem solving in the complex world in which we live.

Education for the Information Age

Patricia Senn Breivik

Now well into 1992, it seems prudent to pause and assess the progress made thus far with the educational reforms initiated in the 1980s. Have any of the issues raised in that decade been resolved, or are the following issues, originally raised prior to the American Civil War, still all too familiar?

    The curriculum is too vocational
    The curriculum is bloated and confused
    The quality of students is declining
    The quality of teaching is poor
    The body of knowledge to be taught in colleges is growing quickly
    The colleges are homogeneous and change is difficult
    The curriculum is out of date
    There are gaps in the curriculum
    School-college relations need to be enhanced
    A safe and democratic society requires quality education
    The society is changing quickly
    Commerce and trade require strong educational programs
    Public confidence in higher education is low
    Other agencies are competing with colleges [Levine, 1986, pp. 50-52].

The only significant difference between the issues of those two reform movements seems to be the influence of the Information Age in which we

---

Portions of this chapter are adapted from the book Patricia Senn Breivik coauthored with Ohio State University President E. Gordon Gee, *Information Literacy: Revolution in the Library,* and from an article prepared for the *AAHE Bulletin.*

now live and in which future generations will live. The Information Age is characterized by rapid exponential growth of new information readily accessible in a diverse mixture of old and new print and electronic formats. Logically, then, it seems wise to look to this new development for a key to better solutions to recurring problems in education. Unfortunately, contemporary education and policy leaders have not seriously thought through the basic curricular implications of the Information Age.

Clearly, campus leaders have not totally ignored the new technology that has come hand-in-hand with the Information Age. Their most visible, curricular response to the information explosion was the acquisition of computer technology. Early on, many campuses encouraged and even required "computer literacy," which in most cases meant learning to program computers. But this initial interpretation of computer literacy was based more on the emotional appeal of popular technology writers than on well-organized analysis of the technology and its role in education, and the limitations of the curriculum changes that it spawned soon became self-evident. Computer software so quickly became user-friendly that, for most people, learning to program a computer was as unnecessary as learning to wire a house for electricity in order to throw a light switch.

Computers are just one source of information; computer technology just one means of storing and accessing information. What students really needed to learn then and still need to learn now is how and when to use computers and how and when to use computer-stored information to solve particular problems. Moreover, almost entirely overlooked in the rush to computer literacy was the potential role of library and media resources and personnel in achieving academic excellence in the Information Age.

Most people would agree that information is power; however, few have stopped to think about how to translate that truism into greater effectiveness in their business, personal, and civic lives. In fact, most people today are information illiterates, and this is having a significantly negative impact on businesses and society in general.

Herbert E. Meyer, a former *Fortune Magazine* editor and vice chair of the National Intelligence Council, underscores the importance of access to and use of good information in the business world in an age characterized by rapid change, a global environment, and unprecedented growth in information resources. Meyer (1987, p. 24) describes the astonishment and growing distress of executives who "are discovering that the only thing as difficult and dangerous as managing a large enterprise with too little information is managing one with too much." While Meyer emphasizes that companies should rely on public sources, which are available to anyone, for much of their information, it is clear that many people in business do not know how to find and use this information effectively. Every day, lack of timely and accurate information is costing American businesses a lot of money.

Given the current economic problems of our country and concerns about America's international competitiveness, the costliness of information illiteracy is ill-afforded nationally and individually. People whose education largely consists of lectures, textbooks, and reading lists are not well prepared for problem solving in the complex world in which they must work. Rather than go to authoritative sources for information needed for decision making, they tend to rely on other individuals who they hope will know more than they do on varying topics. A former U.S. Commissioner of Education summed up the greatest concern of all when he said that there is a danger of a new elite developing in our country: the information elite (personal communication with E. Gordon Gee, September 1986).

The only reform report specifically addressing the issue of information literacy was produced by the Carnegie Foundation for the Advancement of Teaching (Boyer, 1987). In the first release of the report, Boyer (1986, p. 21) states, "The quality of a college is measured by the resources for learning on the campus and the extent to which students become independent, self-directed learners. And yet we found that today, about one out of every four undergraduates spends no time in the library during a normal week, and 65 percent use the library four hours or less each week. The gap between the classroom and the library, reported on almost a half-century ago, still exists today."

Libraries and the Search for Academic Excellence

Seemingly in anticipation of Boyer's (1986) report, the University of Colorado and the Columbia University School of Library Service decided to cosponsor a symposium in March 1987 on the role of libraries in the search for academic excellence. Held in conjunction with the one hundredth anniversary of the School of Library Service, it brought together leaders from higher education and librarianship to explore this issue; Boyer was one of the speakers. The following are some of the recommendations that grew out of the symposium.

> Reports on undergraduate education identify the need for more active learning whereby students become self-directed independent learners who are prepared for lifelong learning. To accomplish this, students need to become information literate whereby they:
>
> - understand the process and systems for acquiring current and retrospective information, e.g., systems and services for information identification and delivery;
> - are able to evaluate the effectiveness and reliability of various information channels and sources, including libraries, for various kinds of needs;

- master certain basic skills in acquiring and storing their own information, e.g., database skills, spreadsheet skills, word and information processing skills, books, journals, and report literature;
- are articulate and responsible citizens in considering current and future public policy issues relating to information, e.g., copyright, privacy, privatization of government information, and those issues yet to emerge.

To make possible the above, information gathering and evaluation skills need to be mastered at the undergraduate level, and learning opportunities should be integrated within the existing departments, analogous to "writing across the curriculum," rather than as stand-alone bibliographic instruction programs. Administrators, faculty and librarians should be engaged in creative new partnerships which transmit to students the value and reward of research in their lives as students and beyond. Information literacy should be a demonstrable outcome of undergraduate education [Breivik and Wedgeworth, 1988, pp. 187-188].

Margaret Chisholm, the then incoming president of the American Library Association (ALA), continued the dialogue concerning the importance of libraries and information technology in accomplishing educational reform goals. To facilitate this dialogue, she established the ALA Presidential Committee on Information Literacy and expanded the agenda to include the K-12 sector. The committee included six leaders from librarianship and the chief executive officers from the Council of Chief State School Officers, the Education Commission of the States, the American Association of Colleges for Teacher Education, the American Association of School Administrators, and School Match.

Although the final report of the American Library Association Presidential Committee on Information Literacy (1989) still has not been read by the majority of librarians, it has been well received by people in education, as well as in advocacy, local government, and business groups. The report succinctly makes the case for the right of all individuals to have access to and the ability to use information to enhance their quality of life, succeed in their work, and fulfill their civic responsibilities. This landmark document in the information literacy effort describes what a school would be like that embraced information literacy as an essential ingredient in an active learning environment, thus preparing students for lifelong learning.

Definitions

The ALA report defines an information literate person as one who can recognize when information is needed and has the ability to locate, evaluate, and effectively use the needed information. It further articulates the means by which people acquire information literacy abilities through a process that moves from passive to active learning. This transition is accomplished by having students assume more responsibility for locating and accessing the material on which they will base their learning. The process is termed *resource-based learning,* and it provides a practical and promising approach to the concerns raised in the reform reports of the 1980s. Instead of relying heavily on textbooks and lectures, resource-based learning prepares students for lifelong learning by having them learn from the wide range of information resources that fill their daily lives, such as newspapers, television, journals, on-line data bases, government documents, experts, and local agencies. In a resource-based learning environment, faculty are facilitators of learning, helping students to learn how to make discerning judgments among the overabundance of data available on most subjects.

Leadership Organizations

The American Association for Higher Education (AAHE) was among the first higher education organizations to acknowledge this emerging issue of the contribution of libraries to academic excellence when it published "Making the Most of Libraries" (Breivik, 1987). Since then, AAHE has established an Action Community on Information Literacy, which is an avenue for ongoing dialogue and programming in this important area.

Moving beyond the efforts of an individual organization, the National Forum on Information Literacy was established in 1989. It is an umbrella group of national organizations committed to helping people become effective information consumers. The majority of members are educational organizations, which range in size from the huge National Education Association to the fifty-two-member Council of Chief State School Officers. In addition to library and educational organizations, such diverse groups as the National Association of Counties, the American Newspaper Publishers Association, the Hispanic Policy Development Project, Information Industry Association, and the National Forum for Black Public Administrators are also members.

K-12 members of the forum are using the focus on resource-based learning as a tool in curriculum reform. The Association for Supervision and Curriculum Development (1991), for example, passed the following resolution:

> Curriculum: Information Literacy
> Today's information society transcends all political, social, and economic boundaries. The global nature of human interactions makes the ability to access and use information crucial. Differences in cultural orientation toward information and symbol systems make the management of information complex and challenging. Current and future reform efforts should address the rapidly changing nature of information and emerging information technologies.

> Information literacy, the ability to locate, process, and use information effectively, equips individuals to take advantage of the opportunities inherent in the global information society. Information literacy should be a part of every student's educational experience.
> ASCD urges schools, colleges, and universities to integrate information literacy programs into learning programs for all.

Certainly, an increase in the number of students who are better researchers and who are comfortable taking on more responsibility for their own learning will have an impact on what faculty can and should expect in student performance. However, the issue of what information abilities students are acquiring as undergraduates needs attention now.

Shifting Paradigms

It is important not to confuse the development of information literacy with library or bibliographic instruction. While campuses with active library instruction programs may have an advantage in incorporating information literacy learning experiences into coursework, there are significant differences between these two areas. On most campuses, library instruction is offered as an add-on to courses and, as such, is usually discounted by students as an extrinsic part of the coursework and, therefore, as irrelevant to the grades that they will receive. Only when faculty require students to use a variety of information resources as part of class assignments do students receive the message that the ability to locate, evaluate, and effectively use information is critical to learning.

The Middle States Commission on Higher Education, a member of the National Forum on Information Literacy, is playing a leadership role in focusing attention on the need for faculty to promote information literacy in the classroom. The commission's efforts are more fully discussed in Simmons (this volume); however, it is worth noting here that a common response at information literacy workshops sponsored by Middle States is that many thoughtful faculty are already, to some degree, facilitating resource-based learning. Nevertheless, there still needs to be a more systematic effort to integrate information resources and technologies into the hearts of the curricula at all institutions. Without this all-out effort, students who have never used an index—much less an on-line data base—will continue to graduate from liberal arts programs.

The individual manifestations of resource-based learning in practice range from the simple to the complex. For example, Victor Fisher, a Towson State University professor, takes a low-technology approach by having students use a telephone conference call to interview leading authorities on Eskimo culture so that they experience firsthand the value of seeking expert opinion in the collection of up-to-date and authoritative information. At

Seattle Central Community College, three faculty members (see McHenry, Stewart, and Wu, this volume) have linked a writing class and a research class to focus on diversity-related issues. Other institutions are beginning to take a more comprehensive planning approach to resource-based learning. Bowling Green University has investigated information literacy and resource-based learning as part of its overall consideration of the role of the liberal arts curriculum, and Samford University has linked information literacy to its concerns for total quality management and core curriculum revision.

As the number of examples of resource-based learning increase, no one seems fully satisfied with the term *information literacy,* especially since it has become associated with scores of claims to fast educational success. Whatever the terminology, however, most information literacy efforts are based on a down-to-earth, common sense approach to moving from mere lip service to actual preparation of students for lifelong learning—a longtime goal of a liberal arts education. Resource-based learning does not require large outlays of new dollars. More computer and multimedia hardware, software, and print material will always be desirable, but students on all campuses can greatly benefit *just* from the integration of existing campus and community resources and technologies.

International Efforts

Efforts directed at producing information literate students are not unique to the United States. In fact, Australia seems to be further along in formal national consideration of this issue. In the National Board of Employment, Education, and Training (1990) report, the entire section "The Library as Educator" deals with issues related to information literacy. One formal recommendation deals with the need for teacher training institutes to include "a formal curriculum element on information skills development," and another deals with the need for reporting on user education programs in annual reports and statistics. A national seminar, "Information Literacy: Australia's Agenda," is planned for December 2-3, 1992. This seminar will bring together leaders from education, librarianship, government, and business.

In 1987, China's central government issued a mandate requiring all academic libraries to provide user instruction to students. Hannelore Rader, director of university libraries at Cleveland State University, spoke on information literacy at Tianjing, Beijing, Chongqing, and Wuhan during fall 1991. She reports that academic librarians were then planning their third national conference on user education. Moreover, as expressed by her contacts in China and Germany, there is, in both countries, a high level of interest in an international conference on information literacy.

In England, the British Library commissioned three studies during the 1980s to determine practices in information skills training. The studies covered universities and polytechnics in both England and Scotland and documented a number of practices that are well worth consideration on American campuses. For example, at Loughborough University in Leicester, faculty guide students through projects in the commercial sector that have students analyze how industry uses information.

The Ultimate Beneficiaries

Resource-based learning provides a practical means of contributing to the long-established educational goal of individualizing the learning process. Common sense dictates that no one instructional approach and no one textbook or reading assignment can be equally effective with all students in any one class. Students come to a class with different levels of academic ability, differences in preferred learning styles, and vastly different interests. When faculty facilitate students' learning from library resources and resources from the broader community, then students can deal with issues closer to their areas of interest while using materials appropriate to their academic abilities and in formats compatible with their learning styles. There is also reason to believe that use of timely real-world resources can increase student motivation. After all, it makes sense that students who use newspapers, television, and on-line data bases will have more immediate and more far-reaching payoffs than can be achieved just by reading about these resources in textbooks.

Ultimately, the beneficiaries of an undergraduate focus on resource-based learning are the students. Repeated learning experiences of identifying, locating, evaluating, and using information to address particular problems will guarantee them quality lives in today's society. Information literacy is not merely a desirable goal but rather a survival skill in the Information Age. It is appropriate, therefore, to end this chapter with the final lines of the report of the ALA Presidential Committee on Information Literacy (1989, p. 10): "To respond effectively to an ever-changing environment, people need more than just a knowledge base, they also need techniques for exploring it, connecting it to other knowledge bases, and making practical use of it. In other words, the landscape upon which we used to stand has been transformed, and we are being forced to establish a new foundation called information literacy. Now knowledge—not minerals or agricultural products or manufactured goods—is this country's most precious commodity, and people who are information literate—who know how to acquire knowledge and use it—are America's most valuable resource."

References

American Library Association Presidential Committee on Information Literacy. *Final Report.* Chicago: American Library Association, 1989. (Single free copies may be obtained by writing to the American Library Association, 50 East Huron Street, Chicago, IL 60611.)

Association for Supervision and Curriculum Development. "Resolution 8: Information Literacy." In *Resolutions: 1991*. Alexandria, Va.: Association for Supervision and Curriculum Development, 1991. (Association for Supervision and Curriculum Development, 1250 N. Pitt Street, Alexandria, VA 22314.)

Boyer, E. L. "Prologue and Major Recommendations of Carnegie Foundation's Report on Colleges." *Chronicle of Higher Education*, Nov. 5, 1986, pp. 16-22.

Boyer, E. L. *College: The Undergraduate Experience*. New York: HarperCollins, 1987.

Breivik, P. S. "Making the Most of Libraries: In Search of Academic Excellence." *Change*, 1987, *19* (4), 44-52.

Breivik, P. S., and Wedgeworth, R. "Discussion Outcomes and Action Recommendations." In P. S. Breivik and R. Wedgeworth (eds.), *Libraries and the Search for Academic Excellence*. Metuchen, N.J.: Scarecrow Press, 1988.

Levine, A. "Deja Vu." *Change*, 1986, *18* (1), 50-52.

Meyer, H. E. *Real World Intelligence: Organized Information for Executives*. New York: Weidenfeld & Nicholson, 1987.

National Board of Employment, Education, and Training. *Library Provision in Higher Education Institutions*. Commissioned Reports, no. 7. Canberra, New South Wales: Australian Government Publishing Service, 1990.

PATRICIA SENN BREIVIK is associate vice president for information resources at Towson State University, Baltimore, Maryland, and founding chair of the National Forum on Information Literacy.

The Middle States Association believes that programs to improve the teaching and learning process should include an appropriate emphasis on information literacy and other resource-based learning strategies.

Information Literacy and Accreditation: A Middle States Association Perspective

Howard L. Simmons

Bibliographic instruction, information literacy, and other resource-based learning programs are extremely important topics for the Middle States Association Commission on Higher Education (CHE). Even though there are differences of opinion about what nomenclature to use and whether the focus should be on bibliographic instruction, information literacy, or resource-based learning, these distinctions pale in importance when compared to the absolute need for all resource-based instructional strategies to be more thoroughly integrated into the teaching and learning process. In fact, the process of increasing the information skills of students and faculty is evolutionary. Moreover, bibliographic instruction, information literacy, and resource-based learning have roles to play in helping students to become more self-directed and independent learners, and faculty to become more effective in helping students to learn how to learn.

One might ask how and why an accreditation agency became such a strong proponent of the centrality of library and information resources in the total scheme of things? And why would an accreditation body link information literacy to the improvement of the teaching and learning process, especially at the undergraduate level? Why is it essential for the Middle States CHE to view bibliographic instruction and information literacy as important factors in the assessment of student learning outcomes and institutional effectiveness?

After members of the Middle States staff and I spent many years extolling the value of lifelong library and information skills, CHE, as a part of its planning process, concluded that one of its initiatives for assisting member institutions in improving undergraduate education should be a stronger emphasis on assessing student and faculty utilization of library and other learning resources. The task of convincing CHE that information literacy is important to the improvement of the teaching and learning process was a relatively easy feat compared to the task of convincing administrators and faculty. More difficult still is the task of convincing faculty and administrators that resource-based learning techniques are not just bureaucratic schemes dreamed up by librarians. And if we are to be successful in getting the message across, we must change some of our basic assumptions about how students should become more information literate, independent learners.

Evolution of Middle States Emphasis on Information Literacy in its Standards

In addition to the glimpse of the Middle States CHE's practices provided by Gelfand (1960), earlier documentation of CHE's emphasis on information literacy and resource-based learning is in *Evaluating the Library* (CHE, 1957, p. 2): "Good teaching and good librarianship [unite] to produce skilled, self-reliant habitual library users." This document suggests that faculty and evaluation teams ask questions such as the following: Is the library providing the instructional, reference, and bibliographic service that students and faculty need to take full advantage of the library's resources? Are librarians closely in touch with curriculum development and faculty planning so that they can anticipate instructional and research needs? These questions are still relevant today, and they address the importance of bibliographic instruction and information literacy as well as the desired relation of information resources in the teaching and learning process.

In the late 1950s, bibliographic instruction programs could be dubbed "orientation" programs, and the closest thing to the application of technological access to information was the public service telephone inquiry. But the range of strategies today includes very sophisticated bibliographic retrieval systems for on-line searches and so forth. Today, library collections are greatly enhanced because of access to many other sources of information in a variety of formats. With respect to the current, more prominent emphasis on bibliographic instruction, information literacy, and other resource-based learning strategies in the Middle States accreditation process, let's examine a brief chronology of the statements included in CHE documents regarding the utilization of library and information resources in Middle States colleges and universities.

In 1920, the standard on libraries (Commission on Institutions of Higher Education, 1920, p. 1) was simply, "There should be library... facilities adequate to the work which the institution announces, and these should be kept up to their full efficiency by means of adequate annual expenditures." Over fifty years later, the standards (CHE, 1971, p. 41) were broadened to include the following statement: "The effectiveness of the library is of paramount importance. Its collections should be appropriate and adequate to support the instructional program, and they should be widely used by both students and faculty." Today, the standards (CHE, 1990, pp. 35-36) are much more explicit in terms of library usage by students and faculty: "Collection development must relate realistically to the institution's educational mission, goals, curricula, size, complexity, and degree level, and the diversity of its teaching, learning, and research requirements. The centrality of a library/learning resources center in the educational mission of an institution deserves more than rhetoric and must be supported by more than lip service. *An active and continuous program of bibliographic instruction is essential to realize this goal.* . . . *Nothing else matters much if the resources are not used*" [emphasis added].

Even though the current standards (CHE, 1990, pp. 34-35) indicate that "a library/learning resources center is of paramount importance to the educational program and to the research of students and faculty" and call for "an active and continuous program of bibliographic instruction," the document *Framework for Outcomes Assessment* (CHE, 1991b, p. 18) moves even closer to the concept of information literacy and the nexus to general education programs. Middle States is interested in the extent to which students master the ability to retrieve and use information. Learning in this area begins in the general education courses and is refined as students move into more specialized curricula. The following questions (CHE, 1991b, p. 18) might be asked about the syllabi for all courses, particularly in the general education programs: "How many syllabi include library assignments? What is the nature of those assignments? Are they appropriate for the program and its students? Do they show evidence of thought and creativity? Do they promote active learning? Do they take advantage of primary sources when appropriate? Do they display a knowledge of the range of resources available to students at the institution? Is there a sense that, as students progress from the beginning of the degree program to its conclusion, they are required to use increasingly complex library research skills?" The recently revised *Designs for Excellence: Handbook for Institutional Self-Study* (CHE, 1991a, p. 41) includes specific reference to "information literacy" to reflect the evolutionary nature of resource-based learning programs: "Of paramount importance in assessing the effectiveness of library utilization is the need in the self-study process to describe and document the strategies and activities used to provide an effective program of bibliographic instruction and *information literacy*" [emphasis added].

CHE further highlights the value of evaluating and assessing the effectiveness of libraries and resource-based learning programs by requesting that all accredited and candidate institutions provide specific information on a variety of library and resource-based learning strategies in their annual institutional profiles, which describe basic institutional characteristics and chronicle changes that have occurred during the previous year or that are projected for the next year. This information is useful to CHE, evaluation teams, and reviewers of periodic reports in determining the evolutionary development of programs and strategies designed to improve students' information skills.

Rationale for an Accreditation Emphasis on Information Literacy and Resource-Based Learning

Because the Middle States CHE is concerned about the continuous improvement of quality, particularly at the undergraduate level, it believes that programs to improve the teaching and learning process in colleges and universities should include an appropriate emphasis on information literacy and other resource-based learning strategies. CHE understands that it has a corresponding responsibility to ensure that this emphasis on information literacy through the medium of the library—as broadly defined—is realized in self-study and evaluation team reports, institutional assessment programs, program reviews, and in accreditation decision making.

CHE's concern about the lack of effective programs of bibliographic instruction and information literacy on some campuses is highlighted in annual reports. Not only are these programs seen to assist students and faculty in making more effective utilization of information sources in the teaching and learning process, but they are also considered to be intrinsically and inextricably related to academic quality and excellence, student learning, teaching performance and effectiveness, and institutional effectiveness.

As educators, most of us today have become increasingly more aware that we and our students need to acquire more sophisticated information skills to access and use information in a variety of formats to address our education and life objectives. We have also become increasingly aware of the role played by computer technology. Even library and information skills can be taught and learned by means of interactive computing. We all know that computer searches are commonplace and that certain data needed for research purposes can be accessed only by means of a computer terminal. And we now depend to an even greater extent on facsimile systems in our use and management of information. CHE is convinced of the need to develop information literacy and resource-based learning programs that involve teaching faculty and librarians in a collaborative way; of the need to get the early support of chief academic officers in the integration of resource-based learning strategies into general education programs; of the need to identify first those administrators who already have a solid commitment to resource-based learning, and those faculty who utilize bibliographic instruction and information literacy techniques; and of the need to develop a reward structure for those faculty whose implementation of strategies result in improved student learning outcomes.

Responsibility for Developing Effective Information Literacy and Resource-Based Learning Programs

It is important to emphasize that all campus groups should be actively involved (including teaching faculty, librarians and other information resource specialists, academic administrators, trustees and presidents, and students) in the development and promotion of effective information literacy and other resource-based learning programs.

Faculty Involvement. Naturally, faculty, including librarians and information specialists, should utilize every means available "to teach users how to take full advantage of the resources available to them" (American Library Association, 1986, p. 196). There is less concern on campuses about what most librarians as teachers will do to implement sound programs of information literacy or resource-based learning than there is concern that many other teaching faculty have little direct involvement in either helping to develop the collections or in ensuring that they and their students make full utilization of existing learning resources. But of even greater concern on some campuses is the inadequate emphasis on the improvement of information literacy and the enhancement of the ability of students to learn independently.

Fortunately, most library instruction programs no longer consist solely of printed brochures designed to introduce patrons to the library, or brief orientation sessions at the beginning of each term for students enrolled in English classes. But even in those institutions that have adopted significant bibliographic instruction and information literacy programs, often too much of the responsibility for improving the students' information skills is placed on the English and communications faculty, primarily through writing-across-the-curriculum programs or through research papers in English classes; the information literacy needs of students is certainly not the responsibility of English faculty alone, and the discipline of English itself does not provide the student with a full range of information strategies.

On the other hand, there are institutions that provide specially prepared courses and program bibliographies upon faculty request, credit and noncredit courses in bibliographic instruction, various forms of computer access to data and on-line searches, group and individualized instruction, telecourses, and special reference services such as "bibliographic service on wheels" to off-campus instructional programs, among others. But those institutions that are seemingly the most effective in getting students to take full advantage of the collections and in promoting the use of resources as a means of improving learning outcomes are also those in which faculty from a variety of disciplines have strong requirements for library research and information literacy built into their instructional programs.

Program requirements, as reflected in course syllabi, student learning contracts, and in the nature and extent of student and faculty use of library materials, give us some indication of faculty commitment to increased effectiveness. When faculty rely almost exclusively on textbooks and make limited or no demands on students to complete library research, it is understandable when students also rely heavily on their textbooks, poorly written lecture notes, and their limited understanding about how to exploit information resources.

Student Involvement. Since the raison d'être of any college or university is the education of its students, no program of bibliographic instruction or information literacy can succeed without students' participation. Students must avail themselves of every opportunity to pursue the truth. They must use the course bibliographies prepared for them by faculty; they must make greater use of reference services; they must make more effective use of existing information in a variety of formats; they should consider taking courses designed to improve their library research skills; and they should make greater utilization of on-line search systems and computer data banks. Students should never be satisfied with an instructional program centered almost entirely on what can be learned from textbooks and lecture notes. In the final analysis, students must become self-directed learners who have mastered the research tools in the search for knowledge and truth.

Administrator Involvement. Academic and student development administrators, in particular, must ensure that there are provisions for easy access to library and learning resource materials by faculty and students. Administrators must be constantly alert to the need for adequate library and other information resources to support current and proposed academic programs.

As part of any overall program for institutional assessment of outcomes, the chief academic officers, working closely with librarians and other faculty, should ensure that adequate resources are provided for faculty and librarian colleagues to acquire appropriate information resources, and that the institution's investment in library and learning resources is utilized. At a minimum, academic deans should ensure that course outlines reflect an expectation for the use of learning resources other than textbooks; should monitor the quality of research papers (including theses and dissertations) completed as partial requirements for course and degree credit, especially in terms of information resources consulted or cited; and should assist faculty in identifying and developing the most appropriate resource-based learning and assessment strategies for their particular programs, courses, and disciplines.

Trustee and Presidential Involvement. Members of governing boards who, according to CHE's (1990, p. 30) standards, are "responsible for the institution's integrity and quality" must view the library as one focus of the effort to maintain and improve quality. Thus, it is the trustees' responsibility, upon recommendation of the president, to provide adequate financial resources to allow the library to develop fully in support of the institution's mission. Presidents should provide leadership in keeping their respective governing boards informed of the important connection between the expenditure of funds for library and information resources and the need to develop information literacy and other resource-based learning strategies that provide the fullest student and faculty access to this significant investment.

Information Literacy and Resource-Based Learning as Essential Factors in the Accreditation Process

In recognition of its limitations, what can the Middle States CHE do as an accreditation body? How might assistance realistically be provided to colleges and universities? CHE hopes to persuade institutions that mission and goal statements should emphasize improvement of students' information skills, and that self-studies not only should reflect an analysis of library collections in relation to the institutions' missions and program offerings but also should provide evidence of a relationship between the objectives of courses and programs of resource-based learning (for example, the actual utilization of learning resources by faculty and students) and student learning outcomes, especially as these relate to the overall quality of the institutions. Naturally, CHE assesses whether or not an institution has adopted appropriate strategies and approaches to improve students' information competencies. While expecting course outlines and syllabi to reflect a strong component of student research and recommended readings, CHE is also concerned that the instructional program is designed to produce more self-directed learners and more qualitative outcomes. For instance, the general education or core curriculum of an undergraduate college might include specific objectives for information competence and research skills.

CHE has come to these conclusions after finally realizing what colleges and universities really mean when they write and speak about the centrality of library and learning resources and their importance in the teaching and learning process. Do such platitudes really mean that there is an understanding of the broader notion of the library as a concept rather than a storage facility? Do the grandiose statements in self-studies, periodic review reports, evaluation team reports, and other documents submitted to CHE really mean that faculty and students are making maximum utilization of library and other information resources? Do faculty and administrators really buy into the notion that effective bibliographic instruction programs can lead to the development of more effective information managers and the development of more self-directed independent learners? Are librarians and information specialists really convinced that they too should be learning facilitators and effective teachers? Can we really believe that college and university administrators are committed to the importance of library resources and their utilization as a part of the teaching-learning process when sufficient resources are not provided to improve collections or access to those collections and other resources? And should the regional accreditation agency really have faith in the documentation of institutional or program effectiveness when the college or university has not assessed quality in relation to questions such as these?

Except in rare cases, the answers to these questions are still essentially negative. As I have stated in numerous presentations before academic audiences, for far too long many of us in the academic community have given lip service to the role of the library as a partner in the teaching and learning process; for far too long librarians—comforted by other faculty and administrator colleagues—have believed that their function is simply to serve as custodians of books and other documents; for far too long faculty have taught courses that demand little more than textbook responses; for far too long faculty have dutifully placed books on reserve without giving full consideration to the impact of this well-accepted but little examined procedure; for far too long students have believed that the only reason for using the library is to prepare term papers; for far too long students have been denied access to or have been generally unaware of bibliographic instruction programs designed to make them more information literate; and for far too long accreditation bodies have been too willing to accept assessments of library effectiveness by institutions and evaluators based almost exclusively on a limited range of input and process measures. The time has come for bolder measures, particularly since some accreditation bodies, CHE among them, have recognized a serious link between library resources and the effectiveness of courses and programs.

Therefore, we must change some of our assumptions about what constitutes a "library" and why accessibility to learning resources and the acquisition of lifelong research and information management skills are important and indispensable elements in quality determination and maintenance. In so doing, I suggest that a partnership of faculty and librarians should work more closely in developing curriculum objectives and assessment strategies. Faculty, librarians, and academic administrators should be alert to the different levels of student information-processing skills when information literacy programs are designed and implemented.

It is absolutely essential that students take some responsibility for becoming more information literate, independent learners. At a minimum, students should avail themselves of resource-based learning strategies, and they should never be satisfied until their learning skills include the most appropriate ways to locate, analyze, interpret, and use information to address academic and life issues. That goal is precisely why CHE's (1990, p. 35) criteria call for "an active and continuous program of bibliographic instruction [or other resource-based learning approach]," and why CHE's (1991b) *Framework for Outcomes Assessment* strongly suggests that all courses require library-based research and information skills objectives. In a recent article (Simmons, 1991, p. 393), I emphasize that regional accreditation bodies, particularly Middle States, have "developed criteria which underscore the importance of bibliographic instruction programs and the results of which might lead to more widespread information literacy." CHE also recognizes there should be greater respect for and commitment to library and information resources as mandatory components of the teaching and learning process.

Impact of Information Literacy Programs on Self-Study and Evaluation Process

Although it is too early to assess what impact current information literacy programs are having on self-study and evaluation processes—particularly since much more interaction with institutions is necessary in terms of setting the agenda for implementation—we do know that consideration should be given to (1) new assumptions about assessing the effectiveness of libraries and their utilization, (2) possible new paradigms for self-studies that emphasize resource-based learning, and (3) how the role of team members and chairs will change relative to the evaluation of the teaching and learning process. For example, we know institutions and evaluation teams will have to do more than focus on the adequacy of collections and library management; CHE will work closely with institutions in the pre-planning phases of the self-studies to determine what other paradigms are suitable for the integration of resource-based learning techniques; and evaluation team personnel will be oriented to the new self-study approaches so that appropriate evaluation strategies will be utilized and recommendations formulated.

CHE will not only expect self-studies to reflect analysis of library collections in relation to the institutions' missions and program offerings but will also expect institutions to reexamine the format and organization of institutional self-studies to ensure especially that evaluations of library resources and assessments of the effectiveness of information literacy programs are not presented as isolated topics with no discernible relation to the teaching and learning process. It is anticipated that future self-studies will present a more coherent view of the teaching and learning process, and better student learning outcomes that are partially the result of information literacy and other resource-based learning programs. In preparing for evaluation team visits and external reviews of the required periodic review reports, CHE will expect institutions to have available course outlines and syllabi that reflect a strong component of student research and information literacy skills.

Moreover, CHE will expect evaluation team members to examine course outlines, syllabi, student research papers, theses, and dissertations; the institution's resource-based learning program; the annual budget devoted to the support of learning resources; and the quality and extent of the institution's collections and of the access to these and other information sources, including those that are required when off-campus programs are available.

Summary and Suggested Directions for Information Literacy and Resource-Based Learning in the Accreditation Process

Each of us needs to be information literate and promote the importance of bibliographic instruction and information literacy as key ingredients in the teaching and learning process. Accreditation bodies such as the Middle States CHE need to go a step further in encouraging the colleges and universities that they accredit to view information literacy and other resource-based learning programs as essential elements in assessing quality, student learning outcomes, and institutional effectiveness.

Clearly, resource-based learning strategies are a part of CHE's broader agenda to place greater emphasis on the total assessment and evaluation of the teaching-learning process and the environment for learning. For too long, self-studies and evaluation reports have been disproportionately attending to issues of management, governance, and communications, as opposed to documenting the outcomes of the teaching-learning process. Likewise, for too long, library and information resource center utilization has been the sole responsibility of librarians. But we are painfully aware today that other teaching faculty, students, academic administrators, presidents, and trustees must begin to collaborate more effectively with librarians and other information resource specialists in ensuring the effective utilization of all learning resources.

Increased emphasis must be placed on the essential collaboration between librarians and other information specialists, academic administrators, and faculty. And if we are to implement effective resource-based learning strategies, librarians in concert with chief academic administrators must be successful in persuading faculty of the benefits of bibliographic instruction and information literacy programs, even when their implementation requires changes in instructional approaches and teaching strategies.

Although most library and learning resource centers have not been able to keep pace with inflation in terms of maintaining collections, let alone provide appropriate support for new programs, the existing resources still represent a considerable institutional investment that is not always effectively utilized. Therefore, it is important that each accredited and candidate institution in the Middle States region develop and implement resource-based learning programs and strategies that are appropriate to students' needs, the nature and level of curricula offered, and available resources within and outside the institution. Institutions preparing self-studies and developing assessment strategies should rethink the manner in which learning resources are to be presented as integral to the teaching-learning process. Evaluators, thoroughly oriented to the increased emphasis on information literacy and resource-based learning approaches in the accreditation process, will be expected to assess the extent to which institutions are making progress in developing programs that help students become more information literate. The Middle States CHE will utilize all of the information resulting from the evaluation and assessment processes to determine how it can assist institutions further in improving the teaching and learning process, especially at the undergraduate level. Quality improvement is still the primary goal of the institution and CHE in the peer review process known as accreditation. Emphasis on information literacy and other resource-based techniques is simply one means to our common goal of ensuring excellence at every level.

References

American Library Association. Association of College and Research Libraries. "Standards for College Libraries, 1986." *College and Research Libraries News,* 1986, 47 (3), 189–200.

Commission on Higher Education. *Evaluating the Library.* Document No. 4.81. New York: Middle States Association of Colleges and Schools, 1957.

Commission on Higher Education. *Policies and Procedures Handbook.* Newark, N.J.: Middle States Association of Colleges and Schools, 1971.

Commission on Higher Education. *Characteristics of Excellence in Higher Education: Standards for Accreditation.* Philadelphia: Middle States Association of Colleges and Schools, 1990.

Commission on Higher Education. *Designs for Excellence: Handbook for Institutional Self-Study.* Philadelphia: Middle States Association of Colleges and Schools, 1991a.

Commission on Higher Education. *Framework for Outcomes Assessment.* Philadelphia: Middle States Association of Colleges and Schools, 1991b.

Commission on Institutions of Higher Education. *Characteristics of Excellence in Higher Education.* New York: Middle States Association of Colleges and Schools, 1920.

Gelfand, M. A. "A Historical Study of the Evaluation of Libraries in Higher Institutions by the Middle States Association of Colleges and Secondary Schools." Unpublished doctoral dissertation, School of Education, New York University, 1960.

Simmons, H. L. "Accreditation Expectations for Library Support of Off-Campus Programs." *Library Trends,* 1991, 39 (4), 388–404.

HOWARD L. SIMMONS is executive director of the Commission on Higher Education of the Middle States Association of Colleges and Schools, Philadelphia. The Middle States Association Commission on Higher Education is a member of the National Forum on Information Literacy.

A vision of quality undergraduate education for the new century has led the Minnesota State University System to emphasize information literacy and to make the library of the future both the locus and the agent for acquiring it.

Linking Undergraduate Education and Libraries: Minnesota's Approach

Linda Bunnell Jones

In 1990, a blue ribbon commission advised the board of directors of the seven public state universities of Minnesota and the people of Minnesota about the quality of education needed to prepare graduates and the state for the challenge of the new century. This group of seventeen distinguished Minnesotans included farmers, corporate executives, labor leaders, public school educators, former legislators, civil rights activists, physicians, hospital administrators, and recent graduates of the universities. They defined the dynamic of the future as "continuing and accelerating change." Indeed, they said that "change should not only be expected, but it may also be the only constant in our lives." They defined the challenge of the universities to be the preparation of graduates to manage change. And they reminded the public "that high-quality education is the strategic resource for Minnesota's future" (Minnesota State University System, 1990a, p. 4).

To ensure that graduates are prepared to manage change, the members of the commission identified what they believed a graduate should know and be able to do. The hallmarks of a quality education, they said, are graduates who can think critically and solve problems, who have a global vision, who have a multicultural perspective, who are scientifically literate, who are ready to work, and who are good citizens and behave ethically.

The commission developed these recommendations after ten months, during which they read research reports and position papers written by faculty. Their deliberations opened with a symposium. They heard Rudiger Dornbusch, an economist at the Massachusetts Institute of Technology, describe the implications of the world's economic future for American higher education (Minnesota State University System, 1990b, p. 6). And they watched as Harold Hodgkinson, the noted demographer, charted the implications of changing demographics for America and Minnesota (Minnesota State University System, 1990b, p. 13). They toured each university where they met informally with faculty and students and visited laboratories and student lounges.

Measuring Success

The commission did not stop with definitions of outcomes to be obtained by graduates. They also thought through how these outcomes might be measured. Much of the last decade in American higher education has been spent debating assessment of outcomes of education. As state legislators listened to requests for more dollars for universities in the 1980s, they asked for evidence that students were learning. In the early phase of the drive for accountability, universities responded by agreeing to test their students to demonstrate what they had learned. Quickly, however, critics pointed out the fallacy of this approach. They noted that examination scores at exit measure what graduates know or can do, not necessarily what a university education contributed to their skills and knowledge. Accountability began to be defined in terms of how far the university could take the students between entrance and exit. And so the definition of testing was broadened to include pre- and postmeasures. Psychometricians cautioned that development of this kind of examination is not as precise a science as some would like to believe. Concern for racial, ethnic, and class bias in examinations raised questions as to how heavily they could be relied on. Many doubted a single measure could demonstrate that a university was discharging its responsibilities to students (Minnesota State University System, 1990b, p. 22).

The commission explored in depth the problem of measuring outcomes. Alexander Astin, a professor at the University of Minnesota, helped them to think of a university education in terms of adding value or developing talent in order to describe the responsibilities of the university (Minnesota State University System, 1990b, p. 26). The commission listened to educators in the states of Tennessee and Virginia who had struggled to implement state-mandated measures of accountability. Finally, the commission proposed the straightforward approach of using multiple performance indicators rather than elaborately constructed tests. They thought of the abilities that they wished to see in graduates to function as citizens and workers and traced backward to think of what would persuade the public, beside test scores, that graduates had these skills and possessed this knowledge. They proposed that performance indicators be developed for each of the seven goals that they had identified. For example, graduates might reasonably be believed to have developed higher-order thinking skills if they completed senior theses or similar integrating projects that could withstand the scrutiny of a jury of faculty and community practitioners. The commissioners gave other examples as well of what, to them, were persuasive performance indicators: (1) study in a foreign country or acquisition of a foreign language and knowledge of the culture as a means of demonstrating a global perspective in articulating the interrelationships of world economics, the environment, geography, history, politics, religion, and the arts; (2) participation in a racially and ethnically diverse learning community as a means of acquiring and demonstrating the knowledge, skills, and values that define a multicultural perspective on social, political, economic, and aesthetic issues; (3) participation in a well-planned, well-supervised field experience that readies a student for the work place; and (4) completion of a community service, citizen participation, or social action project and articulation of the standards of ethical behavior that individuals expect of themselves and of others in personal and professional life (Minnesota State University System, 1990a, pp. 16-20). Although the commission members illustrated what, to them, were persuasive indicators, they urged that each university faculty have the opportunity to identify indicators that it might find more educationally sound or more practicable.

Principles to Observe in the Process

Finally, the commission gave thought to the process that would enable the universities to reorient themselves to achieve the proposed goals and demonstrate their achievement over the next ten years. They relied heavily on the advice of the members of the Minnesota Quality Council, an organization funded by the state originally but now supported by over two hundred corporate and public service members. The council's purpose is to infuse in Minnesota the values of the quality movement in America, manifest in the criteria for the Malcolm Baldrige Award created by Congress in 1988. The Minnesota Quality Council is among the most active in the nation; Minnesota companies, IBM Rochester and ZYTEC, won two of the three Baldrige awards given in 1991.

The commission recommended that the Minnesota State University System adopt the five fundamental principles for achieving increased quality developed by the Minnesota Quality Council (Minnesota State University System, 1990a, p. 5): (1) commitment and involvement in the effort from the top; (2) inclusive participation by all employees of the system; (3) sensitivity to the needs of the external and internal customers of the educational process—the governor and legislative leaders, the public, employers, current students, parents, faculty, staff, and administrators; (4) adoption of "continuous improvement" as a working definition of quality; and (5) continuous upgrading of the knowledge, skills, and abilities of faculty and staff.

Academic Library of the Future

Shortly after the board of directors of the Minnesota State universities adopted the commission's recommendations as the planning tool for the 1990s, an opportunity arose to use the goals defined, the indicators proposed, and the principles adopted in a tangible planning effort. The Minnesota legislature charged the university system with describing the academic library of the future, awarding it $200,000 to complete a report and present schematic drawings by November 1991.

The legislators' action was a response both to the commission's recommendations, which became known as the Minnesota State University System Q-7 Initiative, and to its request for new library buildings on three of its seven university campuses. Two of these buildings had been built or substantially remodeled as recently as 1964. Legislators were concerned that planning for these buildings had not taken enrollment growth, new directions in education, or developments in technology into consideration. They viewed with alarm the prospect of the state funding new library buildings on each campus every twenty-five years.

As the task force appointed by the chancellor began its work, members decided to place the commission's vision of education for the new century at the center of their deliberations. They tried to think about what role the library would play in quality education as defined by the commission. They began to conceptualize the library not as a building but as an environment for helping faculty and students to achieve the goals for undergraduate education. They also saw the library's human and physical resources as means to facilitate students' demonstration that educational goals had been met.

The initial shock was recognition that these ambitious goals for education had implications for the size and depth of collections. If students are expected to acquire a global perspective, they would have to have access not only to printed texts but also to visual media in languages from countries throughout the world. Materials to support the acquisition of a multicultural perspective would also have to be added to print and audiovisual collections. If all students, not just a select few, must acquire a better understanding of mathematics and science, demands for materials in these fields also would grow. If much of what was once laboratory activity could be simulated by computer graphics and video, these materials would have to be stored and equipment for their display provided for students.

In addition to thinking about the new materials and equipment that the library would have to house physically, members of the task force thought through other implications for the university and the library. First, it became clear that achievement of most of the outcomes depended on active rather than passive learning. Students would have to learn and demonstrate what they had learned by doing. The faculty's role would be broader than the tasks of delivering classroom lectures and assigning work for students to do either independently or through use of the materials and personal assistance available in the university library. Faculty would increasingly become mentors or "coaches" to students as students work through their own thought processes rather than the completed thought processes of faculty and authors. Second, it became clear that learning would be more collaborative. Students would have to learn and demonstrate their ability to work with other people to accomplish tasks with both faculty and peers. Third, the process and results of learning would become more public. The tools of communication in the workplace are expanding. Employers communicate to workers, managers, and stockholders using graphs, charts, photographs, and drawings projected technically. Information is presented orally and visually. Indeed, an increasing number of Americans develop their understanding of local, national, and international events by listening to radio and watching television instead of by reading newspapers and magazines. Not only would students need to be taught how to use audio and visual media to communicate effectively, but they also would have to learn how to produce multimedia presentations. They would need a place to prepare these programs and to present them to others.

Members of the task force also considered the impact of technology on the academic library of the future. No other group of persons on a university campus, except perhaps the science and engineering faculty combined, has had to adjust to greater change introduced into the workplace by technology than the level experienced by librarians. Librarians now use computerized data bases instead of card catalogs and periodical indexes to look up information. Materials such as census data for a particular year are no longer available in their entirety in printed form. As members of the task force realized, the sheer volume of information resulting from improvements in technology and the increasing variety of ways in which it is formatted have made it essential for library staff to become more technically adept at searching and teaching others to search and more critical evaluators of sources and materials than has ever before been necessary.

Technology has raised users' expectations for service. Rapid production of multiple copies and facsimile machines have sped the flow of information. Faculty and students have increased appetites for customized learning materials. They have come to demand convenience in delivery of printed materials. Facsimile transmission, use of the telephone, and computer access have made physical distance irrelevant in the learning process.

The Core of Information Literacy

The term *information literacy* has come to summarize the underlying principles of quality undergraduate education for the new century. "Information literacy involves: recognizing a need for information, identifying what is needed, locating it, evaluating it, organizing it, and using it effectively" (Minnesota State University System, 1991, p. A-14). These are the skills that will enable students to manage change. The quality of learning in the future will be more dependent on the quality of the resources that support it. Instead of a faculty member accessing the most current information on a topic and presenting it in lectures, students will need to be able to access all of the materials needed to formulate their own thinking on the topic.

Framework for the Future

After thinking through the implications of their vision of quality undergraduate education for the new century, the task force began working with the Architectural Alliance of Minnesota to create a general framework for the academic library of the future that could be translated into physical and fiscal plans for libraries. The Alliance is an architectural firm, located in Minneapolis, that has a history of planning and designing academic buildings and campuses.

The framework created by the Alliance, based on task force deliberations, establishes priorities in service while broadly defining the library. It challenges previous standards for space, use, and function by tailoring the library to meet the needs of students who are trying to become information literate. It helps universities to plan for library service well into the future without assuming unlimited physical growth in the library. The future of the Minnesota State University System academic libraries entails the following priorities: better libraries, not bigger libraries; access to information resources; and environments for learning and demonstration of learning rather than warehouses for books.

The framework addresses the concern raised initially about the depth and breadth of collection needs to support the goals for graduates. Most of the university library collections today would need to grow substantially to have the materials needed to enhance students' global and multicultural perspectives as well as their scientific literacy. Yet, most of the existing collections have already encroached significantly on the learning environment for students. Books have squeezed out study tables and carrels. Further, collection growth means construction costs that prevent the state and the universities from addressing other priorities. In regard to this dilemma, the task force recognized that "no one library in the Minnesota State University System or in the nation can adequately meet all the demands placed upon it." Access to information has "displaced the idea of ownership particularly on a regional basis." According to task force recommendations, each university should continue to provide immediate access to a collection that supports the basic needs of the curriculum offered at the university, while the libraries of the seven universities—called the Coordinated Collection—will meet more specialized and increasingly diverse information needs. The collection is organized in a single electronic data base under the System's Project for Automated Library Systems, initiated in 1979 and now providing computerized on-line access to the catalogs of the Minnesota State University Libraries and those of many other libraries in the Upper Midwest (Minnesota State University System, 1991, p. 38).

The long tradition of successful collaboration among librarians of the Minnesota State University System and other Minnesota higher education institutions, community librarians, and state agencies provides a foundation for the Coordinated Collection. Minnesota libraries have participated in the Minnesota Interlibrary Telecommunications Exchange (MINITEX) Library Information Network, a state-supported network of academic, public, state agency, and special libraries. MINITEX manages the delivery of needed information by sharing library resources, including collections, bibliographic records, and reference services. This service, combined with the Project for Automated Library Systems, an electronically shared catalog, is tangible evidence of the benefits of collaboration of library leaders in Minnesota.

As a consequence of the reliance on collections located elsewhere, the academic library of the future will devote more space for the patron to search, to request, and to receive materials available elsewhere. In addition, greater space for sending its own materials and receiving those of other libraries will be required.

Given that technology changes rapidly and in ways that are difficult to predict precisely, the library of the future will be constructed with as much flexibility as possible to accommodate the diverse types of equipment needed to access and to display materials in current and future formats. This flexibility may mean added construction costs in the form of electrical wiring, load-bearing walls, and insulation for sound; however, this initial investment will pay off in the long run.

Because Minnesota State University libraries will rely on one another for collection sharing, they will each have more space to devote to students' learning environments. The Architectural Alliance recommends a reversal of the ratio of books to study space from the previous 50 percent for collections and 38 percent for study space.

Study space will include not only space for private reading in carrels or at tables but also sound-proof rooms where students can talk in informal groups. The task force recommends that study space throughout each campus be identified and, perhaps, managed by the library. Certainly, the electronic equipment placed in these spaces should be able to access at a minimum the computerized catalog. Facsimile machines and dedicated telephones to the library should also be in these study spaces, group or private.

The library of the future must have not only space in which to identify, locate, and evaluate information but also space in which to organize information and effectively use it, especially in an era when so much information is expected to be presented visually and vocally. Students need to have access to materials and technical assistance to organize and present information in formats other than the printed word. Faculty, if they are to serve as mentors to students, must have space to view student work at formative stages. In addition, faculty need space and technical assistance to prepare their own classroom and professional presentations if they are to model information literacy for students. Space will be devoted to consultation, education, production supervision, and information presentation. These provisions will enable students to observe as teachers become participants in the learning process and to see librarians and media specialists as resources, not simply custodians of information.

Developing the Report and Creating Change

The means used by the task force to develop the report on the library of the future warrant description here. The Minnesota State University System sought to utilize the five quality principles recommended by the Blue Ribbon Commission. First, there was leadership from the top. The chancellor addressed the task force on several occasions and provided a formal charge. Three of the seven university presidents served on the task force; a retired president chaired it. The vice chancellor for academic affairs for the system was the director. Second, representatives from all constituents in the system participated: graduate and undergraduate students, teaching and library faculty from each university, and deans of colleges or librarians from each. The library deans on the task force were active liaisons with the other deans and directors of libraries in the system. Representatives from community and technical colleges and from the University of Minnesota participated as well. Three librarians from major corporations in the Twin Cities area shared their understanding of employers' expectations for information literacy and their experience in providing services in a rapidly changing environment. Third, the group kept the "customer" at the center of its discussion, defining the customer broadly as the public, employers, current students, returning students, University of Minnesota System faculty, and other universities' faculty and students. Fourth, the task force and library deans and directors committed themselves to continuous improvement. Even though new libraries for three of the universities in the system are a few years away, all deans and directors of libraries are beginning to create the infrastructure for information literacy. Finally, the task force is seeking ways to advance information literacy in professional development for library and teaching faculty. The system's next funding request to the Bush Foundation, a major, private benefactor of the University of Minnesota System, will include a greater focus on the need for new skills in the Information Age, especially within the context of general education and critical thinking.

The Blue Ribbon Commission and the Minnesota State University Board of Directors are beginning to see the impact of their vision of education for the new century not only in the planning for the universities' physical facilities but also, and most important, in the changing approach to teaching and learning.

References

Minnesota State University System. *Q-7: Quality on the Line. A Vision for University Education in the New Century*. Report of the Blue Ribbon Commission on Access and Quality in the Minnesota State University System. St. Paul: Minnesota State University System, 1990a.

Minnesota State University System. *Setting the Stage for the 21st Century: Proceedings of the Q-7 Convocation*. St. Paul: Minnesota State University System, 1990b.

Minnesota State University System. *The Academic Library of the Future*. St. Paul: Minnesota State University System, 1991.

LINDA BUNNELL JONES *is vice chancellor for academic affairs of the Minnesota State University System, St. Paul. She served as director of the Minnesota State University System Task Force on the Academic Library of the Future.*

In the development of information literacy, the teacher's role is to help students learn how to evaluate the information that they find.

An Academician's Journey into Information Literacy

Lois M. Stanford

Learning is in many ways like turning a kaleidoscope. With the turn of the kaleidoscope, bits of colored glass tumble from one pattern into a new and different pattern. The change is irreversible; we can never go back to what was seen before; we can only enjoy the astonishing new pattern and prepare to turn the kaleidoscope again.

So it is also with learning. Aspects of our experience and knowledge and insight tumble suddenly through a paradigm shift into a new pattern, just as do the pieces of colored glass in the kaleidoscope. And as with the turning of the kaleidoscope, learning is irreversible. When learning occurs, we never see the world in quite the same way again.

Components of Experience: Colored Glass Bits

The experience of turning the kaleidoscope happened to me in May 1991, when I was asked to read *Information Literacy: Revolution in the Library* (Breivik and Gee, 1989) and to participate as a commentator in a panel discussion that the book's authors were organizing for the annual meeting of the Canadian Library Association in Montreal. In retrospect, I realize several aspects of my experience were poised for change, like the bits of glass in the kaleidoscope, waiting for the little push that would drop them into a new, more informative orientation—into a new pattern, a new paradigm.

There were three particular components of my recent activities as a faculty member at the University of Alberta—we can call them the green, the blue, and the red pattern pieces—that were loaded and waiting in the kaleidoscope. The green pieces related to my continuing interest in the nature of the teaching-learning process in a university setting, and to my trial-and-error experiments in changing my own classes from formal lecture teaching (passive learning) to activities with greater responsibility shared between myself and students. The blue pieces reflected several years of volunteer involvement in an instructional development project aimed at enhancing teaching skills of university instructors. The red pieces had been newly added to the mix by my recent acceptance of a vice presidential position with responsibility for, among other things, student services in the university; this new job quickened my interest in the kinds of university activities that might improve the quality of students' academic experience, add value to the educational experience, and increase the number of students retained by the institution through completion of their programs.

My reading of *Information Literacy* resulted in these blue, green, and red pieces falling together into a new pattern, a new basis for activity. An analogous event happened to Archimedes in his bath: "Eureka!" Watershed events happen to all of us: exciting experiences that keep us eager learners all of our lives. My transformation began this time during the plane journey to Montreal for the conference, while I read *Information Literacy* and wondered what I would say during the panel discussion. As it turned out, I had plenty to say!

Information Literacy and Instructional Development: Blue Glass Ruminations

Changes in how faculty and students view teaching and learning have their roots in the shifting realities of the worlds in which they work, learn, and live.

The Shared Responsibilities of Teaching and Learning. While I read *Information Literacy,* I reflected on my experience several years earlier when I worked as a faculty volunteer in the instructional development project mentioned earlier. During the program, colleagues and I talked about new notions. The training for our careers had been in specialized academic domains, and the idea that the art of classroom teaching could be more than the skill of delivering a good lecture developed surprisingly slowly in some minds.

Gradually, members of the group began to view teaching as the facilitation of learning. Yeats was quoted: Education is "not the filling of a vessel, but the lighting of a fire." We talked about a deemphasis on information transfer and a new emphasis on teaching students how to learn, about not giving a fish to a hungry person but rather teaching that person how to fish. New methods of instructional delivery were investigated. We read, and talked, and experimented; we consulted again with colleagues when our experiments showed that we had more to learn. We persevered, because we were finding out for ourselves that teaching and learning are a shared responsibility, that students must learn (and teachers must teach them) to be resourceful team players. We had never heard of the notion of information literacy, but we espoused, for sound pedagogical reasons, one of its basic principles: student self-reliance.

If, during that project, we had had a copy of *Information Literacy*, it would have provided a framework for our ideas about teaching enhancement. Resource-based learning makes effective and efficient use of what each party, teacher and student, brings to a university course, and the notion of a teaching-learning contract with understood responsibilities on each side greatly enriches and enlivens the activity of university teaching.

The Importance of Instructional Development in Today's University. Instructional development, and the concomitant interest in instructional techniques that are effective, efficient, and individualized, is an important facet of the needs of the academic institution today for a number of reasons. Let me list four that constitute a general litany of university woes (or challenges) in this final decade of the twentieth century.

The Crowded Campus. In Canada, we have a very large number of students enrolled in universities and colleges, more than our facilities were designed to accommodate. Every year the number rises as the job market shrinks; every year we have more students to instruct. We have quotas in faculties such as arts, science, and education, which in the past have been open to any student who met the academic standard. These quotas foster a competitive atmosphere, which in itself tests our teaching skills.

Diminishing Resources. It is probably true that no university has ever been appropriately funded to meet all or most of its needs. Nevertheless, the past few years have been extraordinarily lean, and the trend shows no signs of reversing. In terms of our teaching responsibilities, we have seen seminars turn into small lecture courses, and small lecture courses into large ones, often with fewer colleagues to teach them.

Increasingly Heterogeneous Student Body. The last decade has seen an astonishing enrichment of the types of students in our universities. We have more mature students, more students from abroad, more physically challenged students, more students who work full- or part-time, more students who are single parents, more aboriginal students, more transfer students, and more students who enter from nontraditional high schools. This diversity is of great value in ensuring a rich intellectual broth for the university, but for the teaching faculty it poses a challenge of varied student preparation and varied student needs to be addressed in a single course.

The Student as Consumer. Increasingly, students view themselves as consumers of the university's product, and increasingly they voice their needs as consumers. They, and the society that they represent, are no longer content to take what they get and say thank you to the academy. They ask to take some responsibility for their journey into the educated life, for which we should be glad, and for which we must take responsibility as teachers. It occurred to me, on the plane journey to Montreal, that a university instructional-development center—which is what our early efforts at teaching improvement at the University of Alberta actually evolved into—might be well advised today to use the notions of information literacy as a basis for developing in the faculty the range of skills required to overcome the formidable array of challenges that we now face.

A Case History of Information Literacy in the Classroom: Green Glass Actions

As I ruminated on the advantages that an information literacy orientation could supply to initiatives for improving and enhancing university teaching skills, I realized that several years ago I had, quite unwittingly, put an elementary form of information literacy into practice in one of my own classes. Here, then, is the case history of my own initial steps toward teaching in an information literacy framework. This experience supplied the green glass bits in my metaphorical kaleidoscope.

I was scheduled to teach, for the third time, a senior linguistics course on the social and psychological aspects of second-language acquisition to thirty students—a mix of undergraduate senior linguistics majors, master's candidates in education specializing in the teaching of English as a second language, and graduate student teaching assistants from the modern language departments who were actually doing foreign language teaching in the real world. Overall, this was a highly motivated group with very diverse and practical interests in the course material.

I had taught the course during the previous two years in a lecture format. I liked to lecture; student evaluations suggested that I did it fairly well. But since I had been thinking and talking about self-directed learning, I decided in the third year of the course that I had better practice what I was preaching. The class and I discussed the matter thoroughly: They recognized the wealth of varied experience that they brought to the group, and they recognized the diverse goals that they hoped to achieve in the course. Everyone bought into the idea of self-directed learning; everyone knew what she or he would be expected to accomplish during the term. It was agreed that I would lecture half of the time, and the other half would be devoted to independent or small group initiatives. We began the term flushed with enthusiasm and in good rapport.

Very shortly, however, we discovered that old habits die hard. Students began to long for their full classes of lecture; the task of absorbing lectures was easy learning, passive and reassuring. I missed lecturing. I could not believe that the students would not suffer if they did not hear everything I had talked about in previous years. I doubled my speed of delivery. We reassessed.

Armed with knowledge of our weaknesses, we recommitted ourselves to our path of self-directed learning. But students were unsure of their skills. "Give us a bibliography," they said; I did, and they limited themselves to that bibliography. I gave them a journal list, and they looked no further than those journals. Finally, I asked, "Where do *you* think you might look for reliable literature?" And once the right question was asked, those clever students hot-footed to the library to ask the experts—the librarians!

The needed partnership was therein established. The library became co-teacher, and the course became not only self-directed but rooted in the resources that students would need to know how to use in their professional lives. The role of the classroom teacher then appropriately became one of helping students learn how to evaluate the information that they find and how to fit it into their developing frameworks of knowledge. The class had become information literature.

The experiment was a success. Students were rewarded for their perseverance by learning, and by developing new skills for lifelong professional learning. The instructor was rewarded for her perseverance by learning even more than did the students.

Information Literacy and Student Services: Red Glass Plans

The last bits of colored glass, the red pieces, were added to my kaleidoscope through work in the area of university student services. Student services, in my view, consist of those activities, facilities, and safety nets that enhance the quality of student life and learning, enrich a student's academic endeavors, and increase the university's rates of student recruitment, retention, and degree completion. Student services are functions that add value to the student's primary academic undertaking.

On the plane to Montreal, my reading of *Information Literacy* suggested to me two areas in which the information literacy philosophy of education could march with the goals of student services. These were recruitment and retention of the excellent student, and retention and success with the at-risk student. As well as explaining my past experiences to me, *Information Literacy* was pointing the way to new ideas and goals.

Recruitment and Retention of the Best. Competition among universities to attract the outstanding student is keen. How are such students to be brought to the table? What can a university offer that will attract these students and turn them away from competitors?

The new pattern in the kaleidoscope suggested to me that the offer of an education based explicitly on skills for the twenty-first century might be powerfully attractive bait. And what skills would one advertise? *Information literacy for an information society.*

Retention and Success with the At-Risk Student. The demand for university education from an increasingly heterogeneous population and the university's social responsibility to offer its resources to the nonstandard student suggest that in the future we will see more students who are at risk of failure. These students may find themselves inadequately prepared for university work, or laden with family or employment responsibilities. An information literacy framework for education can provide an opportunity for the partnership of instructors and librarians to remediate and enrich the standard university fare to the advantage of these students.

Two examples of concrete initiatives by which to address these twin goals of retention and success with at-risk students suffice to illustrate the new sorts of student services that can be provided within an information literacy framework—the productive assimilation of students and their microcomputers into the campuswide information systems and an information literacy focus for a "first-year experience" course to orient students to university work.

Students, Microcomputers, and the Campus Information Network. Students in increasing numbers arrive at universities with their own microcomputers. Instructors in increasing numbers make use of instructional software to enhance their teaching. University computer centers accept as a major responsibility the provision of instructional computing laboratories; newer versions of these laboratories allow students to "dock" their own microcomputers at a central server. Students so docked can access the library and, through it, a rich variety of data bases, classrooms, and public computer information networks across the campus and across the world. To use this world of wonders responsibly and productively, students must be information literate; the university must decide who is to take the responsibility for making them so: the library and the classroom instructor are the logical team. With the assistance of this team, students' opportunities to learn increase exponentially.

Students' First-Year Experience. Many universities are beginning to investigate the utility of a first-year experience course, the purpose of which is to orient students to university education and to increase their success rate in their encounters with the academic life. The concept of this type of course was first developed by John Gardner at the University of South Carolina; in Canada, the University of Prince Edward Island and the University of Victoria are pioneers in the field (Upcraft, Gardner, and Associates, 1989).

The University of Alberta sees great value in developing a course of this kind. What better focus for it than information literacy? What better methodology than resource-based learning?

In a large multiversity, this type of course might usefully be based in the individual faculty and make use of the special subject area library. Events move quickly: At present, the University of Alberta libraries have already taken a first step along this path. The medical librarians are now offering to first-year medical students a six-week course titled Information Literacy in Clinical Medicine.

Conclusion

The turn of the kaleidoscope that occurred for me when I read *Information Literacy* formed a new and informative pattern from my experiences with students and with learning. This new pattern cannot be undone. It will continue to inform my actions until I turn the kaleidoscope again and the now familiar pattern becomes the basis of yet another new design.

References

Breivik, P. S., and Gee, E. G. *Information Literacy: Revolution in the Library.* New York: American Council on Education and Macmillan, 1989.

Upcraft, M. L., Gardner, J. N., and Associates. *The Freshman Year Experience: Helping Students Survive and Succeed in College.* San Francisco: Jossey-Bass, 1989.

LOIS M. STANFORD is vice president of student and academic services at the University of Alberta, Edmonton, Canada.

The effort required to start and keep resource-based learning projects running is amply rewarded by the skills that students gain and the improved products of their efforts.

Natural Partners: Resource-Based and Integrative Learning

John R. Porter

Much has been written recently about information literacy and bibliographic instruction and the necessity for incorporating these skills into college curricula (Bodi, 1990; Breivik and Gee, 1989; Coleman, 1986; Moran, 1990; Nahl-Jakobovits and Jakobovits, 1990). These discussions provide a good rationale and a theoretical basis for the development of projects and programs to facilitate student use of bibliographic resources and integration of the attendant concepts and skills into curricula. Some literature also addresses particular aspects of information literacy programs, such as use of the computer for on-line searching by students (Brundage and deFur, 1989; Penhale and Taylor, 1986). A search of the literature yields comparatively few examples of the integration of these principles and practices into assignments for specific courses, especially those developed or implemented by the primary course instructors. Some recent examples include a program for general education courses (Selin, 1988), a project in foreign language classes (Maloney, 1989), and a few programs in biology courses (Blystone, 1989; Hotchkiss and Nellis, 1988; Stachacz and Brennan, 1990). The need for additional examples and models is clear.

Although term papers and other writing exercises have long been assigned in the college classroom, the majority of these are described in syllabi with little other than general topic, page length, format, and due date. This was the tradition at Philadelphia College of Pharmacy and Science until about 1985, when an Earlham College presentation on bibliographic instruction suggested alternative approaches to training students in the techniques of acquiring and organizing information. Since that time, some of the biology faculty have formed a partnership with the library faculty and staff in the development of assignments that teach the tools necessary to access information and are meaningful within the context of the respective courses.

Freshman Projects at Philadelphia College of Pharmacy and Science

The approach adopted initially for use with freshman students was the original term paper concept to which was added training in the use of *Biological Abstracts, Index Medicus,* and the subject index of *Science Citation Index.* Although the quality of papers improved significantly, there still was considerable frustration expressed by students because of their inexperience with the scientific literature, as well as by faculty because of the time required for grading the fifteen hundred to three thousand pages of writing produced. Term papers continue to be, with some modification, the assignment of the biology course designed for health science majors and nonmajors.

The frustration expressed by both students and faculty seemed justified, and so a literature assignment was designed that allows students to become familiar with the scientific literature without being overly burdened with an in-depth understanding in their first exposure; this project also has been easier to grade. It was adopted in the freshman biology course designed for biology, chemistry, and biochemistry students.

Literature Search. In this assignment, presented during the first semester, freshmen choose a topic from a prescreened list that emphasizes biological themes with a nonmedical focus. Although this emphasis represents the personal biases of the biological sciences faculty, the belief was that the majority of students are more familiar and comfortable with medical topics and so are more likely to be superficial in their coverage without realizing the complexities of the particular topics selected for the literature searches. Medical topics are also less likely to expand the students' awareness of the breadth of biology and current areas of research. Using *Biological Abstracts, Index Medicus, Biological and Agricultural Index,* the subject index of *Science Citation Index,* and the card catalog, students develop bibliographies of ten primary journal articles and two books relating to their respective topics. Each student is also provided with a questionnaire related to a model journal article on firefly predation by spiders (Lizotte and Rovner, 1988). The questionnaire requires students to recognize and describe the species and taxonomic position of the organisms mentioned in the paper as well as the focus and major results of each of the experiments done by the authors, analyze a specific table of data, and compare the quantitative and qualitative data presented in the paper. The development of the bibliography and completion of the questionnaire constitute the entire assignment for the first semester of the course. The grade for this assignment is based on the responses to the questionnaire, the relevance of the bibliography to the topic chosen, and the choice of primary articles (those written directly by the researchers whose work is being reported), rather than secondary works (reviews, books or chapters with broad coverage, or popularized articles). While secondary sources can be valuable for understanding a research area, the primary article includes both the original data and the original interpretations of those data. These may be missing or used in a significantly different context in secondary articles.

Understanding the Literature. In the second semester, each student rereads the materials listed in the bibliography compiled in the first semester, writes original abstracts for two of the articles on that list, and also writes a summary paragraph on the state of knowledge about the chosen topic. Assistance in the construction of abstracts and the understanding of articles is given in either the lecture or laboratory portions of the course as appropriate. The students are also assigned a supplementary text, *A Handbook of Biological Investigation* (Ambrose and Ambrose, 1987), which includes instructions for the construction and understanding of each of the elements of a scientific article, including the abstract; there are also chapters on statistics, graphics, and computer use in the preparation of laboratory reports, term papers, or articles for publication. Unlike the *Council of Biology Editors Style Manual* (Council of Biology Editors Style Manual Committee, 1983), this supplementary text is designed for students rather than practicing professionals. The focus of the assignment for students is to understand and assimilate the information contained in a small body of scientific literature.

Senior Projects at Philadelphia College of Pharmacy and Science

The senior projects are designed to familiarize students with the intricacies of the research process, from the selection and narrowing of a topic through the final stage of presenting their results at professional meetings.

Literature Update. The senior, and some junior, biology and biochemistry students have the experience of resource-based learning reinforced in a cell biology course. These students are exposed again, or for the first time in the case of most transfer students, to bibliographic sources with the addition to the whole of *Science Citation Index, Current Contents*, and the on-line data bases MEDLINE and Biosis. Each student learns how to conduct an on-line search. *Current Contents* is a weekly publication of the Institute for Scientific Information, in Philadelphia, which publishes the tables of contents of selected journals in each of seven series. Cell biology students most often use the life sciences and the agricultural, biological, and environmental sciences issues, although there are also issues that focus on clinical medicine; physical, chemical, and earth sciences; engineering; technology and applied sciences; social and behavioral sciences; and arts and humanities. This exercise is therefore usable in courses in a variety of disciplines, not only the biological or natural sciences.

The emphasis of this assignment is on development of up-to-date awareness of the literature covering particular topics. The topic of the assignment for each student comes from a "citation classic" contained in each issue of *Current Contents*. Citation classics are articles that have been judged seminal to particular areas of investigation based on the number of times that each has been cited in the literature. The text of the classic is usually an interview with one or more of the original authors who explains the motivation behind the original research, problems encountered, and research that has been pursued since the original article was published.

With the help of librarians, I compile, once a year, a list of twenty to thirty citation classics that are related to some aspect of cell biology. Each student chooses a separate classic and derives a topic from a reading of that article. The topic chosen does not have to be the focus of the article but must be derived in some way from it and maintain the study angle of the cell and cellular processes.

Because cell biology is a graduate preparatory course, the assignment is designed to clarify the process that a graduate student would use to decide on an appropriate topic for research. First, our student must search the literature on this topic for the prior two years. The topic choice is then refined during the search to yield a final, up-to-date list of thirty to fifty citations. From this list, the student summarizes ten of the articles with original abstracts. Each abstract must show the relevance of the article to the chosen topic and summarize the major methods, results, and conclusions as they relate to the chosen topic. *A Handbook of Biological Investigation* (Ambrose and Ambrose, 1987) is also assigned as a supplementary text for this course, with reference for this assignment to the sections on abstract preparation. (The other parts of the book are used in the preparation of laboratory reports for the course.) Because Philadelphia College of Pharmacy and Science is in an area with a wealth of academic and professional libraries nearby, and because students rarely explore these other facilities even though they complain of the inadequacies of a small institutional library with a health science focus, at least two of the articles abstracted must be from journals inaccessible at our college but available in these other libraries.

When students receive an assignment for a term paper, bibliography, or other library-oriented exercise, they often wait until just shortly before the due date to begin work. It is also generally true that the due dates for term papers come at or near the end of the semester, coincident with preparation for final exams. For these reasons, only six weeks are allowed for the completion of this exercise and the due date is in approximately the middle of the semester.

The grading of this assignment occurs in three phases. First, the lists and abstracts are examined for style, adherence to formats and other guidelines, and relevance of the abstracts to the topic chosen. An on-line search is then conducted on MEDLINE using the student's statement of the topic as the key words. Even though some of the topics have a nonmedical focus, there is usually sufficiently broad coverage to allow a brief search of nearly any cellular subject, even those concerning bacteria, fungi, plants, and invertebrates. The results of this search are the basis for assessing the completeness of the updating, the breadth of the topic chosen, and the absence of plagiarism from the published abstracts. This is not a complete search to find every paper that the student identified, but a quick search to get a sense of the student's work. If just one or two additional articles are found, the list is fairly complete; but several to many additional articles indicate a lack of effort, imperfect search strategies, or improper narrowing or expansion of the original concept. A sufficient number of the student's abstracts are checked against the originals to ensure that plagiarism of the original authors' words or style has not occurred. Finally, the list of abstracted articles is checked against the library's serial holdings list to determine whether the student followed the instructions to use sources found in other libraries.

Preparation for Oral Presentations. The ability to convey the essence, data, and relevance of a body of literature to an audience is just as important as the ability to find that information in the library. This communication skill is the focus of the biology seminar course for seniors. In the past, when biology seminar students were required to give a single, final seminar presentation, the result was usually a stumbling, poorly organized review of topics well below the level of the average freshman biology text. Students had been given little instruction and this was apparent in their presentations. The department faculty decided to improve the quality of the seminars so that the course would be a worthwhile experience for both the students enrolled and the faculty attending the presentations.

Senior biology majors in the seminar course now have an experience similar to that of the cell biology students with respect to instruction on use of resource indexes and on-line search techniques. Seminar students also learn principles and techniques of copy preparation for overheads and slides and how to use computers for word processing and graphics and various lettering machines and graphics packages available at our Learning Resource Center. Before the first student presentation, instruction is given on a range of topics, including the appropriate breadth of topics for short presentations (twenty to fifty minutes in length), the effective use of slides and transparencies, and the preparation of quality graphics for poster presentations.

The seminar assignments are in the form of poster sessions and seminars developed from searches on topics chosen by each student. The only limitation on topics, other than a biological focus, is that clinical investigations must generally be avoided; these studies frequently lack a hypothetical base and present data that do not lead to clear interpretations or conclusions (for example, "of ten patients who received a drug, two died, one moved away, four got better, and three are being studied further").

Posters are included in the assigned projects because they constitute the most common format for the presentation of research results by beginning and intermediate graduate students at local, regional, and national professional meetings. The poster includes an abstract, introduction, materials and methods, results, discussion, and references, just as found in a journal article, but the emphasis is on concise language, minimal detail, and a presentation that visually conveys the research conducted. The poster is designed to be both a brief summary of a specific research project and a catalyst for discussion between the presenter and audience. The seminar students present these posters to their faculty and peers and answer questions. They are assessed on their preparation, clarity, visual orientation, and attention to the details of both informational content and poster preparation mechanics.

A major emphasis in other assignments is the quality and appropriate use of visual aids in the presentation of data and concepts to increase the effectiveness of oral presentations. Within a few days after the presentation, the student meets with the instructor to discuss the student's own impression of the quality of his or her presentation, the comments received from peers and faculty through evaluation forms completed at the end of each presentation, the major strengths and weaknesses of the presentation, and the areas most in need of attention in preparation for subsequent presentations.

The results of this approach have been remarkable. Several students each year give very professional and clear presentations. All students show consistent improvement from the first presentation to the last, and only very rarely is even the first seminar as poor as the average final seminar given before these modifications to the course were instituted.

Often, several students are enrolled in both classes, cell biology and seminar, simultaneously. These students do not have to duplicate their efforts, but they learn the same techniques in both courses. Because the focus of the assignments and the nature of the finished products in each course are quite different, the students may freely use the same techniques and even the same topics in the two courses.

Motivations, Rewards, and Disappointments

The design and implementation of these resource-based assignments grew out of a desire to improve the quality of students' educational experiences. These changes in teaching style have not all been easy, but they have produced important benefits for students and faculty, despite some student and faculty resistance.

Benefits. These assignments have increased the amount of interaction between the biology and library faculty as well as satisfied the primary goal of giving the students the tools needed to use the resources of the library effectively in the context of specific tasks. The freshmen are introduced to the scientific literature and learn the rudiments of how to access, read, and understand it. The senior students apply these skills in developing literature bases in specific research fields. The greatest reward for me is when students return from their first year in graduate school to report that they have impressed their major advisers with their abilities to do thorough literature searches in very little time, and that they have been able to move very quickly into new research based on their knowledge of the pertinent literature.

The benefits to the two departments involved in these projects include recognition of the Department of Biological Sciences as a leader on campus in providing educational experiences that greatly assist students and recognition of the willingness of library faculty to work with other faculty in the design and implementation of meaningful assignments that enhance library and bibliographic search skills and information evaluation skills within the context of specific courses. Faculty in the institution as a whole benefit in having students better equipped to do useful searches of the literature and to understand the materials read. The college also benefits in that the graduated students are better able to compete in postbaccalaureate studies, whether academic or professional, as well as in the technical workplace. These alumni are more likely to value their educational experiences when they can see that their achievements have been made possible in part by the resource-based learning skills acquired in college.

Disadvantages and Disappointments. Our approach to helping undergraduate students achieve information literacy is not for those who want instant gratification. Students have grumbled about these assignments, just as they do about most of their coursework. Most do not realize the utility or the power of their skills until required, following graduation, to demonstrate them. Even among the faculty there is a failure to understand how these projects specifically address the skills required to successfully access and acquire information. For example, one faculty comment that I received during the first year of the cell biology project was that this was "no big deal, a lot of faculty assign term papers."

It is clear that the introduction of resource-based learning projects into courses that do not have library-oriented assignments will require greater time and effort than will be needed for those courses in which term papers and similar exercises are the norm. However, the amount of time required is not much different from that needed for a normal term paper, even though the benefits to the students are much greater. The amount of organization required at the beginning of the project is greater, but the grading time is less than required for the average, poorly written, poorly researched term paper. The effort expended thus far to start these projects and keep them running over the last few years at our college has been amply rewarded by the skills that the students have gained and the improved products of their efforts.

Not all of the faculty share this feeling. Faculty colleagues have been encouraged to adopt similar projects, or to develop projects that dovetail into the overall effort to increase students' information literacy. Something resembling the cell biology project in the junior year would allow the seniors to build on their skills to produce high-quality finished products such as research proposals or review papers. It is disappointing that most instructors have not adopted a similar approach largely because of perceived or real changes in time commitment to this one aspect of the total education process.

References

Ambrose, H. W., III, and Ambrose, K. P. *A Handbook of Biological Investigation*. Winston-Salem, N.C.: Hunter Textbooks, 1987.

Blystone, R. V. "Enhancing Science Courses with BI: Three Approaches." *Research Strategies*, 1989, 7 (2), 55-60.

Bodi, S. "Teaching Effectiveness and Bibliographic Instruction: The Relevance of Learning Styles." *College and Research Libraries*, 1990, 51 (2), 113-119.

Breivik, P. S., and Gee, E. G. *Information Literacy: Revolution in the Library*. New York: American Council on Education and Macmillan, 1989.

Brundage, C. A., and deFur, P. L. "Teaching Biology Students On-line Literature Searches." *Journal of College Science Teaching*, 1989, 18 (4), 240-241.

Coleman, P. "Give 'Em the Big Picture: Bibliographic Instruction for Freshman Orientation." *Research Strategies*, 1986, 4 (3), 132-135.

Council of Biology Editors Style Manual Committee. *Council of Biology Editors Style Manual: A Guide for Authors, Editors, and Publishers in the Biological Sciences*. Bethesda, Md.: Council of Biology Editors, 1983.

Hotchkiss, S. K., and Nellis, M. K. "Writing Across the Curriculum: Team-Teaching the Review Article in Biology." *Journal of College Science Teaching*, 1988, 18 (1), 45-47.

Lizotte, R. S., and Rovner, S. J. "Nocturnal Capture of Fireflies by Lycosid Spiders: Visual Versus Vibratory Stimuli." *Animal Behavior*, 1988, 36 (6), 1809-1815.

Maloney, Y. "Bibliographic Instruction for Foreign-Language Classes: A Pilot Project." *Research Strategies*, 1989, 7 (2), 61-66.

Moran, B. B. "Library/Classroom Partnerships for the 1990s." *College and Research Library News*, 1990, 51 (6), 511-514.

Nahl-Jakobovits, D., and Jakobovits, L. A. "Learning Principles and the Library Environment." *Research Strategies*, 1990, 8 (2), 74-81.

Penhale, S. J., and Taylor, N. "Integrating End-User Searching into a Bibliographic Instruction Program." *RQ*, 1986, 26 (2), 212-220.

Selin, H. "Teaching Research Methods to Undergraduates." *College Teaching*, 1988, 36 (2), 54-56.

Stachacz, J. C., and Brennan, T. M. "Bibliographic Instruction in an Undergraduate Biology Course." *Research Strategies*, 1990, 8 (1), 14-21.

JOHN R. PORTER is associate professor of biological sciences and research associate professor of medicinal chemistry and pharmacognosy, Philadelphia College of Pharmacy and Science.

It is no longer sufficient for faculty to teach what they know best.

Teaching Resource-Based Learning and Diversity

Kelley Emmons McHenry, J. T. Stewart, Jennifer L. Wu

Our proposal is to teach resource-based learning and information literacy in the context of cultural pluralism. Does this sound like wishful thinking or idealism run amok? Given the current challenges to the academic canon and pedagogies, faculty and librarians at Seattle Central Community College feel fortunate to have created a linked model of two courses that integrates these elements. Moreover, we believe that this linked model can be replicated or adapted at other institutions. In this chapter, we examine our underlying assumptions, present the conceptual framework for the courses in the linked model, and suggest possible institutional challenges to the use of this model.

Definitions

As we worked to create our linked model, we agreed on these principles: research supports writing and writing supports research, writing instructors need the specialized help that librarians can provide, and cultural pluralism needs to become an integral factor rather than an added-on curriculum unit. Continuous dialogue and research are the basis of our consensus on the following definitions:

Resource-Based Learning. Resource-based learning goes beyond classroom lectures and textbooks to draw on a wide range of information sources and formats, both within and outside libraries.

Information Literacy. Information literacy has four components: (1) an attitude that appreciates the value and power of information, (2) an awareness of the diversity of information forms and formats, (3) an understanding that information is not necessarily knowledge until it has been analyzed, questioned, and integrated into the existing body of knowledge, and (4) a process to access and assess information critically and effectively (Gratch, 1991).

Cultural Pluralism. Cultural pluralism is a state of equal coexistence in a mutually supportive relationship within the boundaries of one world of people of diverse cultures, with significantly different patterns of beliefs, behaviors, colors, and languages. To achieve cultural pluralism, there must be unity within diversity. Individuals must be aware of and secure in their own identities, and they must be willing to extend to others the same respect and rights that they want for themselves (Coalition for Cultural Pluralism, n.d.).

Using Resource-Based Learning and Information Literacy to Teach Cultural Pluralism

Cultural pluralism can and should be a part of all curricula in all disciplines; subjects have evolved within the human context of real-life, cultural parameters. For example, at Seattle Central Community College, an Ethiopian student and a native Seattle student may have different concepts of time. From this empirical observation, we can fashion a critical question: How can the concept of time be described in two countries, Ethiopia and the United States? The process of answering this question can lead students to mathematics, history, astronomy, and so forth. They will discover that diverse cultural perspectives and values can be found in each discipline.

When cultural elements are integrated with learning about skills-based subjects such as bibliographic research and writing, and this learning takes place within the social context of small learning communities, the process becomes more meaningful for both our students as learners and ourselves as educators. When we humanize our pedagogy in ways that make us define and examine our own cultures in relation to other cultures, we also increase our understanding about each other as human beings.

A model linking resource-based learning and an academic or professional discipline (in this case, composition using documented papers as its focus and library research methods) provides an excellent context for exploring cultural pluralism. Three components help to establish the necessary setting:

Instruction. Effective instruction requires a commitment from faculty and librarians to cultural pluralism and a willingness to work together as partners. Those involved need to be able to establish a classroom atmosphere of cooperation and trust. As they deal with course content and information retrieval, they need to develop and encourage provocative questions and assignments.

Library Collection. The library collection must represent diverse cultural perspectives and histories and provide resources that support cultural pluralism inquiry. A multicultural collection communicates to students that all cultural groups have valuable interests and perspectives. Bibliographies and exhibits that highlight this collection can stimulate all students to investigate cultural pluralism topics. Faculty and librarians should work actively to build and maintain a library collection that represents the full range of diversity.

Learning Community Experience. This is a teaching strategy that uses, whenever possible, small group projects to foster social and academic learning. When classes are taught in tandem, students spend more time with each other and build stronger personal relationships and academic collaboration. Linked courses provide coherence and a relationship between subject matters and hierarchies of skills. If the class is fortunate to have a culturally diverse student population, it will have a greater number of resources to tap. Preliminary findings suggest that the learning community experience not only provides positive social reinforcement to participants but may also enhance their academic performance (MacGregor, 1991).

The Linked Model at Seattle Central Community College

Seattle Central Community College is a small, urban two-year college located close to the downtown area. The campus has a diverse population of about eight thousand students, 36 percent of whom are of minority ethnic origins. The college also has the largest hearing-impaired and interpreter program on the West Coast, with over five hundred deaf students. An additional dimension of the diversity of the student body is reflected in the following statistics: 35 percent work full-time, 19 percent are responsible for children, and 56 percent enter with prior educational experience.

Within this environment, we revised two college transfer courses—English Composition 102 (five credits) and Library 101 (three credits)—and created a model that links their content of documented writing and library research methods. Students are required to enroll in both classes, which meet during a two-hour block. Although faculty and librarians work as a team, the classes are taught separately but scheduled back-to-back. Enrollment is limited to twenty-five students. When the linked courses are advertised to students, we explain our purpose in terms of our expectations for students: "Thinking as a Writer, Thinking as a Researcher—Putting it All Together." The students are to think of themselves as practicing writers and researchers whose audience is composed of their peers.

Conceptual Framework. The conceptual framework is based on the following elements: learning as process; problem solving; critical questions; strategies for writing by focusing on audience, occasion, and purpose; strategies for research by developing the ability to recognize and use information systems; logic of information and documentation systems; use of the computer for inventing and generating topics and for writing, editing, and information retrieval; learning communities; and nontraditional assessments of student learning. Using this framework, faculty and librarians planned the linked courses according to a common outline: (1) Cultural Pluralism and the Power of Information, (2) Academic Disciplines and the Classification of Knowledge, (3) Evaluation of Information Resources, (4) Computers and Research, and (5) The Right to Information and How to Protect It.

Evaluation. Evaluation is a continuous process. Instructors evaluate students using self-assessment, oral presentations and class participation, group exercises, bibliographic research projects, assignments designed to explore research processes and strategies, and documented research papers using the Modern Language Association or American Psychological Association guidelines. They also assess student learning through classroom research strategies. In particular, instructors look for evidence of student progress in three areas: multicultural literature and knowledge of diversity, critical thinking, and lifelong learning skills.

Assignments. Instructors design assignments using multicultural themes and concepts in all units. Students are encouraged, but not required, to choose research topics on cultural pluralism. Examples of past topics chosen by students are "Black Politicians: A Comparison of Marcus Garvey and Malcolm X," "The Influence of Japanese Art on Impressionism," and "Deaf Culture in America." The practice of showing students sample information formats is one of the easiest ways to integrate cultural pluralism. Also, multicultural reference books exist in almost every subject area and provide examples of the standard format.

If students are learning about encyclopedias, atlases, handbooks, or dictionaries, instructors can introduce them to *Gallaudet Encyclopedia of Deaf People and Deafness* (Van Cleve, 1987), *We the People: An Atlas of America's Ethnic Diversity* (Allen and Turner, 1988), *The Negro Almanac: A Reference Work on the African American* (Ploski and Williams, 1989), or *Dictionary of Mexican American History* (Meier and Rivera, 1981). If they are learning citation formats and annotation writing, instructors can use sample annotations from *Asian American Literature: An Annotated Bibliography* (Cheung and Yogi, 1988). Each student is provided with short bibliographies in the humanities, social sciences, and sciences that contain examples of reference books in each of the most common organization formats, including a variety of sources relevant to particular ethnic groups.

Guest speakers are utilized in the linked courses to bring new elements of diversity into the classroom, not only by virtue of their professional backgrounds but also as members of underrepresented ethnic groups. They can act as both role models and stereotype breakers. One example is a small press publisher who talked about her specialty, African American books, and the importance of small press publications as sources of alternative or nonmainstream information. Audiovisual resources are also utilized and integrated with classroom exercises and assignments. For example, students view *The Road to Brown* (California Newsreel, 1989), a documentary about the court cases leading to the Supreme Court's 1954 landmark decision *Brown v. Board of Education,* which ruled segregated schools unconstitutional. Students are asked to list pieces of information that can be supported with printed documentation. Then, in small groups, they create research strategies for finding the supporting documentation and for identifying useful resources in the college's library.

Textbooks with a sufficient range of multicultural material are extremely difficult to find. Unfortunately, this difficulty applies also to research-based anthologies designed for reading- and writing-across-the-curriculum programs. Therefore, each quarter we put together our own supplemental text containing readings, reference bibliographies, guidesheets, and exercises. Instructors have found excellent suggestions for group activities in Mensching and Mensching (1989) and Fink (1989).

Significance and Relevance of the Model

Hill (1991) describes the American higher education system as, in large measure, dysfunctional with respect to the following factors: the information explosion, rapid social change, extraordinary diversity of perspectives and standards, conflicting expertise, and increasingly complex intellectual and public policy issues. It is no longer sufficient for faculty to teach what they know best. They need to empower students by providing them with the skills needed to keep up with changing ideas from a wide range of viewpoints and to navigate through complex data bases and information overloads.

Most libraries and publishing houses are still dominated by white, middle-class values. Many heroes and much of the history of ethnic groups are either not represented or are devalued in textbooks and reference materials. The college curriculum must be inclusive. Multicultural experiences and perspectives should be cast in an equal and positive light that encourages students of color to succeed. Emily Style provides an appropriate and vivid metaphor: "Education needs to enable the student to look through window frames in order to see the realities of others, and to look into mirrors in order to see her/his own reality reflected" (Brewer, 1990, p. 6).

Banks (1988) identifies four levels of multicultural curriculum reform that reflect different levels of integration of ethnic content: from lowest to highest, the contribution approach, the additive approach, the transformation approach, and the social action approach. Faculty and librarians at Seattle Central Community College redesigned courses for the linked model to help students reach the transformation level, which enables them to view concepts, issues, events, and themes from the perspectives of diverse ethnic and cultural groups. This goal was accomplished by providing a constructive and safe environment for inquiry, exploration, and dialogue.

Strategies for Replicating the Model

At Seattle Central Community College the impetus for creating the linked model in the context of cultural pluralism came from external as well as internal forces and resources. Federal Title III grant money for the project and anticipation of the state legislature's impending mandatory outcomes assessment testing constituted the external forces. The internal forces came from the students. A series of racial incidents directed against students of color (in this case, Asian Americans) led to the formation of a student coalition, reminiscent of the black studies movement several decades ago. Students, who were joined by faculty, asked that diversity be reflected in the hiring of staff and faculty and in the curriculum. As a result of these internal and external forces, many activities were initiated, funded, developed, and implemented, including the revision of the courses in the linked model.

Before change can occur, faculty—indeed, the institution as a whole—must be aware of the need for change. Sometimes, this need must be created. Without the external and internal factors noted earlier, the context of cultural pluralism might not have been chosen for the revision of courses in the linked model. Frequently, change can be unsettling since it is seen as a threat to one's field of specialty and to one's established curriculum and way of teaching—in short, to one's territory. From a traditional perspective, librarians are not expected to teach the process of writing, or to know what goes on in composition classrooms. Similarly, faculty are seldom encouraged to know much about the library except as a place to send their students or to put books on reserve. Indeed, some faculty notions of research-based writing may involve outdated library systems that have not incorporated any of the new information technologies.

Creation of a climate for innovation presupposes an institution's commitment to change and a clear vision of its future. Change cannot be accomplished simply through wishes. There must be a specific strategy for making change happen. To introduce resource-based learning and information literacy in the context of cultural pluralism, the following steps need to be taken: (1) Explore funding and staffing, (2) determine long-term or short-term commitments, (3) foster awareness of cultural diversity, (4) encourage faculty and librarians to work together as equal partners, (5) establish alternative models for collaboration, (6) promote writing and research across the curriculum, (7) design classroom research projects on current writing and research practices, and (8) provide incentives for faculty and students to participate in the revision process.

Benefits of Integrating Learning

Central Seattle Community College's information literacy program creates an atmosphere in which diversity is valued. It helps to legitimize everyone's place in our society. It also helps improve the self-image of minority students and builds a bridge of understanding. In addition to putting a positive focus on these values, this approach fosters student interest in cultural pluralism as an academic pursuit. For example, when students do annotated bibliographic work and accompanying critical studies on topics such as the Harlem renaissance or contemporary Japanese American poets, they are following their own interests and contributing to scholarship that may have been neglected or is just emerging.

Moreover, the practice of integrating learning develops a cooperative learning and teaching climate. Instruction improves when faculty share ideas, resources, and a sense of process. Students learn to work effectively in groups, but, most of all, they become responsible for their own learning; and they love it. By focusing on a variety of academic disciplines, faculty see how writing courses can transcend what might be considered a traditional "literature major" bias and provide a vehicle through which diversity is respected and integrated into the curriculum and students can determine their own information needs and become immersed in resource-based learning.

In constructing and teaching courses in the linked model at Seattle Central Community College, the faculty and librarians are meeting successfully the challenge presented by the Association for Supervision and Curriculum Development (1991): "Information literacy, the ability to locate, process, and use information effectively, equips individuals to take advantage of the opportunities inherent in the global information society. Information literacy should be a part of every student's educational experience." And to this definition of information literacy we have added cultural pluralism as a requirement for the health and survival of democratic institutions in America.

References

Allen, J. P., and Turner, E. J. *We the People: An Atlas of America's Ethnic Diversity.* New York: Macmillan, 1988.

Association for Supervision and Curriculum Development. "Resolution 8: Information Literacy." In *Resolutions: 1991.* Alexandria, Va.: Association for Supervision and Curriculum Development, 1991. (Association for Supervision and Curriculum Development, 1250 N. Pitt Street, Alexandria, VA 22314.)

Banks, J. "Approaches to Multicultural Curriculum Reform." *Multicultural Leader,* 1988, *1,* 9-12.

Brewer, C. "Minority Student Success in College: What Works." *Washington Center News,* 1990, *4,* 4-11.

California Newsreel. *The Road to Brown.* Videocassette, 47 min., 1989.

Cheung, K.-K., and Yogi, S. *Asian American Literature: An Annotated Bibliography.* New York: Modern Language Association, 1988.

Coalition for Cultural Pluralism. *Cultural Pluralism.* N.p., n.d.

Fink, D. *Process and Politics in Library Research: A Model for Course Design.* Chicago: American Library Association, 1989.

Gratch, B. "Information Literacy." In C. Doyle (comp.), *Quotes and Definitions from Information Literacy.* Towson, Md.: National Forum on Information Literacy, 1991 (Photocopied).

Hill, P. J. "Who Will Lead the Reform of Higher Education? Librarians, of Course!" *Washington Center News,* 1991, 5, 3-8.

MacGregor, J. "What Differences Do Learning Communities Make?" *Washington Center News,* 1991, 6, 4-9.

Meier, M. S., and Rivera, F. *Dictionary of Mexican American History.* Westport, Conn.: Greenwood Press, 1981.

Mensching, G. E., and Mensching, T. B. *Coping With Information Illiteracy: Bibliographic Instruction for the Information Age.* Ann Arbor, Mich.: Pierian Press, 1989.

Ploski, H. A., and Williams, J. (eds.). *The Negro Almanac: A Reference Work on the African American.* Detroit: Gale Research, 1989.

Van Cleve, J. V. (ed.). *Gallaudet Encyclopedia of Deaf People and Deafness.* New York: McGraw-Hill, 1987.

KELLY EMMONS MCHENRY *is a librarian and instructor at Seattle Central Community College. She has worked as a librarian in Kenya.*

J. T. STEWART *is an African American poet and playwright. She teaches in the Humanities Division and the Video Arts Program at Seattle Central Community College.*

JENNIFER L. WU *is a librarian and instructor at Seattle Central Community College. She has lived and worked extensively in Asia, Brazil, and Nigeria.*

As an ongoing experiment and an evolutionary process, the information literacy program at King's College requires us to change tactics and strategies as we learn from our own experiences and the experiences of others.

Information Literacy and a College Library: A Continuing Experiment

Judith Tierney

This chapter chronicles the evolution of the information literacy program at King's College in Wilkes-Barre, Pennsylvania. As an ongoing experiment, we continue to learn from our efforts. From the lessons of experience have come insights and improvements in the program. Our current program and its successes are built on the foundation of our previous missteps and achievements.

King's College has for many years recognized information literacy as a skill of paramount importance to college graduates if they are to successfully meet the challenges of living and working in the twenty-first century. The core curriculum identifies information literacy as one of eight transferable skills of liberal learning that King's students are expected to master. The eight transferable skills are a combination of traditional liberal learning abilities and new technological skills.

Competence Growth Plans

A distinctive feature of the curriculum is the use of faculty-designed competence growth plans for each of the transferable skills of liberal learning. These plans provide students with guides for developing the skills, beginning at a generic level in the core curriculum and concluding with specific applications in advanced coursework within the major. These growth plans specify not only sequential learning objectives relating to skill development for students from freshman through senior years but also strategies embedded in a variety of courses that help students meet these objectives. The plans also identify assessment criteria for judging students' progress and provide bases for specific feedback to students. Each growth plan concludes with a statement indicating the competence level expected by the faculty in a student's major prior to graduation.

Faculty enhance and refine a student's information skills throughout all four years of study. The fruit of this developmental process is evaluated, for the last time, by faculty in the senior seminar courses required in all major programs. Senior seminars require students to engage in projects or original research and frequently to present their work publicly.

With only five librarians available, classroom faculty have to play a major role in assisting students. The library and librarians cannot be all things to all people. Generic bibliographic lectures "on demand" are discouraged in order to conserve library resources and concentrate on advanced instruction. The librarians are convinced that information skills need to be taught within a meaningful course context, that is, as an integral part of a course rather than an add on. The goal is to improve students' knowledge of their subject areas through improved information skills. While faculty are not in a position to teach "the library," they are in a position to introduce and use information skills to teach in their respective subject areas.

Study Guides

To facilitate the faculty's work, the library has developed a growing series of study guides. These guides are designed to be used by students alone or as part of a class assignment. The study guides cover a variety of topics, ranging from how to write abstracts and annotations to how to analyze the quality of information sources. These guides are popular because of their flexibility. The study guides, adapted from other colleges and universities such as the University of Texas at Austin, Cornell University, and Emory and Henry College, make it easier for faculty to incorporate and use information skills in their classes and assignments. With the study guides, annotated bibliographies, critical analyses of articles, and other alternatives to term papers have become more meaningful and more frequent assignments.

Freshman Program

As a first step in implementing a curriculum-based literacy program, the reference librarians developed a self-paced workbook to be completed as a requirement of the core course on effective writing taken by all incoming students. The workbook was designed to introduce students to basic research sources and strategies and to the library. Similar discipline-specific workbooks were later developed for use in introductory courses in education and biology. Each of the workbooks was to be reinforced with research projects assigned by cooperating faculty, who required in their courses the use of the resources and strategies introduced in the workbooks.

Our experience with the workbooks has been enlightening. In theory, workbooks provide a common learning experience for the target student group with minimal staffing, but our pre- and posttesting led us to conclusions similar to those reached by Pennsylvania State University in the assessment of its workbook program (Ware and Morganti, 1986): For many students, learning is marginal at best. Student evaluations of the workbooks were overwhelmingly positive, but experiences with students at the library reference desk supported the test findings that information and skills acquired through completion of the workbook exercises were not transferred to actual research projects.

In an effort to address some of these perceived deficiencies, the general workbook was redesigned into a freshman library project that requires students in the targeted core courses to select a topic and follow it through a sequence of basic resources, just as they would follow the steps of a research strategy. It is our hope this version of the basic project will provide a more realistic research experience and result in better scholarship. Early indications are that some faculty have effectively incorporated the project into their courses and assign supporting research and writing exercises. Since faculty commitment to resource-based instruction is crucial to its success, this project is being monitored and evaluated.

Advanced Research: Phase 1

The second stage in our efforts to devise a curriculum-based literacy program centered on discipline-specific components. Orientations, workbooks, and other general programs introduce students to basic strategies for information gathering, but not to resources and methodologies unique to specific disciplines. While faculty requests for individual bibliographical instruction sessions in specific courses or class projects partially address this issue of information literacy in specific disciplines, the result is often haphazard. Students in some majors learn about resources available to them but none of them has systematic, sequential preparation for advanced research in their fields. It is probable, given the rapidly changing landscape of information, that some instructors are unaware of much of the information that is now available and do not design their research projects to give students experience with both the old and the new resources in their disciplines. To overcome this gap, it is necessary for librarians to work closely with faculty at the design stage of the research modules for their courses.

Initially, we envisioned advanced discipline-related instruction using the vehicle of a single course required of all majors in a particular field, similar to the program at Western State College of Colorado (Jacobson, 1987). Two courses were selected to test this approach: Computer Applications in the Social Sciences, required of all majors in the Social Sciences Division, and Principles of Marketing, required of all marketing majors.

Librarians met with the faculty teaching these courses, discussed the research components of the courses, suggested modifications to enhance their research value, produced annotated bibliographies and study guides, and conducted library sessions to support student research.

The social sciences students are required to select topics related to their major fields, research the topics in both print and computerized resources, and produce position papers and partially annotated bibliographies on the subjects. Although no pre- or posttesting has yet been conducted on this project, the cooperating faculty members report an improvement in the quality of student research. The marketing students are required to devise marketing plans for products of their choice and prepare extensive written and oral presentations of their plans, which follow a prescribed format. The marketing plans require students to identify the economic, social, political, and business environment in which they will be marketing their products. Students need information not only about their respective companies and products but about their competitors as well. Students also may need cultural information to anticipate consumer reaction to their products. Demographics and data on distribution networks are required also. In some cases, students also must design and present advertising campaigns.

Our experience with this phase of our information literacy program brought the realization that it is too much to expect students to learn all aspects of specialized research in one course. Just as students acquire knowledge of the content of their disciplines in a cumulative manner, through a sequence of courses, the process of learning the literature of a discipline logically follows a similar pattern, one layer at a time. An undergraduate majoring in a particular field ordinarily will first take an introductory course that surveys the breadth of the discipline, then a number of specialized courses that explore in more depth the component parts of the discipline, and, finally, as a senior, a seminar or capstone course that brings together or draws on the myriad skills, information, and knowledge accumulated throughout the undergraduate experience. We conclude that the path to information literacy should parallel as well as interconnect with the path to undergraduate mastery of discipline content.

Advanced Research: Phase 2

Our goal is to provide all students with instruction in the literature of their respective major fields, in a sequence roughly paralleling instruction in the content of the fields. For this phase of the experiment, librarians examined the major programs offered at the college and selected human resources management, the study of the management of people in the workplace, as a starting point. There are several reasons why this program was selected. It is a relatively new major at the college with a manageable number of students and a faculty open to new approaches and ideas. The interdisciplinary nature of the field demands proficiency with a wide range of resources, both those specific to human resources management and those in the cognate disciplines of psychology and business administration. Students and practitioners of human resources management must be adept at research in all of these areas.

After holding discussions with human resources management faculty and closely examining departmental course requirements and syllabi, we selected several courses for the information literacy program because of their special content and instructional opportunities, in addition to the introductory and capstone courses required of all majors. For instance, the psychological assessment course necessitates the use of psychological resources; personnel training operates within the context of educational literature; study of the legal environment of human resources management requires the use of legal materials such as federal and state laws, court cases, regulations, and other government documents; analysis of organizations exposes students to the literature of business; and the study of compensation and benefits enables students to focus on resources peculiar to human resources management.

The first semester of this project involved three courses: Introduction to Human Resources Management, Compensation and Benefits, and Techniques of Psychological Assessment. We discussed research modules with the human resources faculty before the semester began, prepared annotated bibliographies and study guides to support their assignments, and conducted library sessions for the students.

In one course, students scan the classified sections of national, regional, and local papers to identify occupational related trends. Students record their daily observations in journals. Once they identify potential patterns, such as increased demands for health care workers, students use a variety of library resources to seek out background information on their observations. Students are asked to identify potential reasons for their findings, explain the trends that they have found, and place them within a larger social, economic, and political context. This assignment of putting numerous observations together to spot trends and identify possible explanations and relationships is close to the real-world work of human resources professionals. This inductive approach is difficult for many students because they are accustomed to working from a deductive position in courses with well-established topics or events. Even with instruction, students have difficulty getting used to the inductive approach. However, the instructor is pleased with current results and notes the more extensive use of citations and the improved quality of analyses in students' final reports.

At the semester's end, we met with the faculty to assess our progress and plan for the next semester. At this point, we are relying on faculty perceptions of improvements in students' work, faculty reports of student comments and behaviors, and our own observations of changes in student and faculty behaviors to gauge the program's effectiveness.

Lessons Learned

Observations of the operations and results of the information literacy program provided us with opportunities to learn from our efforts. Implicit assumptions were challenged, and unintended consequences gave us insight into the vital contribution of the program.

Faculty Interest. It is a truism that bibliographic instruction must be course-embedded and relevant to students' proximate needs. To adapt the expression of George Santayana, those who cannot remember this fact are doomed to relearn it. The need for relevance means that information literacy programs are intensely dependent on faculty, and our experience has been that individual and collective faculty commitments are wavering commodities. Faculty have many things drawing on their time and attention, and it is rare to find many faculty who place information literacy anywhere near the tops of their priority lists. As a result, the consistent investment in time for careful and frank discussion, planning, execution, evaluation, and reworking, which a sound bibliographic instruction program needs, is not always forthcoming from faculty. Serious commitment cannot be mandated from above, or at the college, division, or department levels; it must ultimately be a grass-roots phenomenon, worked out by faculty in collaboration with librarians. It requires constant monitoring, careful nurturing, and time. It also takes time to establish mutual trust between the two groups.

Staff Time. One of the greatest enemies of a good information literacy program is time, not only the time of faculty but also the time of librarians. In many libraries, professional staff have multiple responsibilities. Our staff of three reference librarians provides reference desk services sixty-eight hours a week, performs on-line searches, and provides bibliographic instruction. One of the reference librarians is also the collection development librarian; another has assumed responsibility for planning and administering a local area data base network; the third provides access and research assistance to the college archives and special collections. Add in committee work, meetings, professional development, and the other activities that are part of the normal operations of an academic library, and little time is left for the serious thought and effort required for an effective literacy program. The shortage of time has considerable impact not only on the existence and quality of an instruction program but also on the nature of the program. For example, with our present staffing, to provide for the information literacy needs of upper-level students, we cannot conduct a staff-intensive program for first-year students. This limitation led us to select the self-paced workbook and its successor as vehicles to introduce students to library resources, since they require a limited investment of staff time. Staff limitations are ever in our minds as we face the challenge of building an overall program for information literacy.

Nurturing. An information literacy program can never be considered a "done deal," nor can any of its component parts. It is always in a state of flux and requires constant nurturing and attention. What works for a semester or year or several years will not continue to work indefinitely. Faculty tend to be idiosyncratic, and what works with one faculty member will not necessarily work with another. Students' needs change. Technology is ever-changing. Ongoing research gives us greater insight into how students become information literate. Recent research indicates that the traditional tool-specific approach to learning how to do research is not the most effective strategy (Kohl and Wilson, 1986). In a sense, we are involved in an ongoing experiment, an evolutionary process, and must be prepared to change tactics and strategies as we learn from our experiences and the experiences of others.

Technology. The explosion of new technology—integrated automated systems, on-line search services, compact disk data bases, local and wide area networks—presents us with additional responsibilities and opportunities. We have the responsibility to provide students with access to computerized searching and with instruction in its appropriate use. The ability to automatically monitor how students use computerized sources provides us with a new means of gaining insight into their research methods. We pale when we discover that someone has used the *Modern Language Association Bibliography* to find information on the Coca Cola Company or the *Social Sciences Index* to find literary criticism on Jonathan Swift. We painfully come to the realization that students prefer inappropriate computerized data bases to appropriate print sources. Life in the library, for both users and librarians, has become, simultaneously and paradoxically, simpler and more complicated. Technology has made it dramatically evident that students' abilities to do effective research are intimately bound to their abilities to think clearly, and we must discover ways to deal with this fact in our instruction programs.

The proliferation of technology and the need to teach students how to fashion searches to fit their own information needs to the specific protocols and idiosyncrasies of individual data bases have also made it clear to us that students require detailed hands-on instruction in order to become effective data base searchers. To that end, we have begun planning an instructional facility and network within the library from which we can access all of our data bases and give students hands-on instruction without inconveniencing others who need to use the same resources.

Assessment. How do we assess the impact of instruction on students? What outcomes do we want to measure? What tools do we use? Which results do we believe if we use more than one kind of measure and receive contradictory information from them? We can continue to test students' ability to answer tool-specific or strategy-specific questions, as we have done traditionally. Or we can measure students' feelings about their own ability to do research and to use the library, as is done at Stockton State College (Trail and Gutierrez, 1991). Or we can follow the lead of those who evaluate student bibliographies to assess the effectiveness of bibliographic instruction (Ackerson, Howard, and Young, 1991).

With our freshman workbook program, we used two types of assessments: an objective test that measured student improvement in selecting and interpreting tools and strategies and a subjective questionnaire in which students rated their own experiences with the workbook and attitudes after completing it. These two assessment instruments produced conflicting sets of results. Consequently, as with other components of the program, we now base our evaluation on feedback from involved faculty and on our own experiences with students at the reference desk. Although all of these methods have some validity, we are still searching for an evaluation tool that can measure the effectiveness of the total program and each of its components parts.

While learning is difficult to measure, our observations indicate changes in attitudes and behavior. Historically, libraries have served a social function for college students, and King's College is no exception. However, the library's entrance turnstile count is down 14 percent since 1983; and while observers are seeing less purely social interactions and gatherings, other measures of library activity have grown precipitously. Circulation has increased 64 percent, journal use is up well over 95 percent, and use of reference materials has increased over 100 percent. Student and faculty use of the interlibrary loan service has grown 125 percent since 1983. Faculty with no previous working relationship with the library often help themselves to library-produced study guides and distribute them in their classes.

While students are using the library less as a study and gathering place and more as a research service, the information literacy program alone cannot take credit for these changes. There is no denying that program assignments affect library usage. But this connection should be viewed within the context of other curriculum and campus changes. Student use of the library is closely tied to faculty and their teaching methods. Changes in how students and faculty use the library are not linear or predictable. On a day-to-day basis, change is frequently so minimal as to be unnoticeable. But over a longer period and perhaps from different vantage points, progress is observable.

Conclusion

The evolution of the information literacy program at King's College has not been without its difficulties. Then again, change within an academic environment is seldom smooth. Because faculty are an integral part of the process, librarians must encourage and reinforce faculty efforts until these efforts become an inherent part of their teaching. Over the history of the project, the expectations of librarians and faculty have been adjusted more than once. Perhaps there will always be a gap between the ideal and the real. However, lasting change does not come overnight; it is negotiated and renegotiated one element at a time.

Sometimes, we feel that we are still at the beginning stages of our pursuit to implement the best information literacy program for our students. It is a pursuit marked by progress and setbacks. Occasionally, there are unexpected and unintended outcomes and consequences. Much hard work and learning is ahead of us, in terms of both our own efforts and the efforts of others. The current and future information needs of our students, who will live in the twenty-first century, demand that we accept the challenge.

References

Ackerson, L., Howard, J., and Young, V. "Assessing the Relationship Between Library Instruction Methods and the Quality of Undergraduate Research." *Research Strategies*, 1991, 9 (3), 139-141.

Jacobson, F. "Issues in the Implementation of an Information-Gathering Competency Requirement in Business." *Research Strategies*, 1987, 5 (1), 18-28.

Kohl, D., and Wilson, L. "Effectiveness of Course-Integrated Bibliographic Instruction in Improving Coursework." *RQ*, 1986, 26 (2), 206-211.

Trail, M. A., and Gutierrez, C. "Evaluating a Bibliographic Instruction Program." *Research Strategies*, 1991, 9 (3), 124-129.

Ware, S., and Morganti, D. "A Competency-Based Approach to Assessing Workbook Effectiveness." *Research Strategies*, 1986, 4 (1), 4-10.

JUDITH TIERNEY *is associate professor and reference librarian at King's College, Wilkes-Barre, Pennsylvania.*

If it is important to help students achieve information literacy in small colleges, can large universities afford to do otherwise?

Information Literacy at Universities: Challenges and Solutions

Marvin E. Wiggins

Many professors are seeking ways to enrich their students' learning. There are obvious limitations to textbook instruction and what a professor can personally convey in a classroom. An alternative is to bring students to the informational resources available in the library. Research papers are assigned with a hope that students will discover the variety of resources available, broaden their understanding of the topic, and learn to select and to apply information most appropriate to their needs. Their effort is frequently frustrating, both to them and to their professors. Students find too much information, are not prepared to evaluate information critically, seek to prove what they already believe, and treat the research paper only as a product to be produced rather than a process from which to learn.

Information Literacy at Small Colleges

Professors and librarians are increasingly working together at small colleges to develop students' information literacy. Earlham College in Richmond, Indiana, provides an excellent example of this cooperation. Earlham's faculty regularly plan with librarians to develop programs that enrich the curriculum; they have developed course-related and course-integrated library instruction in most of their academic departments. Yet, Earlham is a small college.

Robert Johnstone, professor of political science at Earlham College, wanted to help his students understand the legislative process of passing bills. He believed that the most effective learning would result from having students visit Washington, D.C., and follow a bill through all the steps to passage. But since a first-hand visit was not possible, he wanted to go beyond lecturing on the legislative process, with textbook and other readings as supplements, to a method by which students could actually trace a bill through all of the steps. Johnstone contacted the librarian at Earlham and together they devised an assignment that would accomplish this task. Students not only gained an appreciation of how a bill is passed, but they also learned how to use U.S. government documents (Farber, 1984).

When professors and librarians work together, student learning is enriched. Librarians know sources and strategies to access information, and professors best understand the subject content and can help students evaluate and apply information. The possibilities are unlimited. Professors usually require students to obtain a background for their topic, identify the issues, select the more reputable sources for examining those issues, trace references cited by authorities, collect and evaluate what they find, and make appropriate application of that information. Many would argue that unless students learn such skills, they will not be able to make informed decisions in their professional and personal lives.

The Challenges at Large Universities

At the university level it is much more difficult, if not impossible, to reach every student. Faculty are more independent and frequently approach their courses as autonomous units in the curriculum. A university may have twenty or more libraries, including an undergraduate library, a graduate library, and several specialized libraries. How does one coordinate instruction among such libraries, let alone reach in an organized manner the seventeen thousand students at Northwestern University, or the twenty-five thousand students at the University of Illinois, Urbana, or the fifty-four thousand students at Ohio State University? Many universities cite their sizes as a reason for abandoning information literacy objectives. But if it is important to help students achieve information literacy in small colleges, can large universities afford to do otherwise? Many universities have looked at their situations and found solutions. Although their levels of success differ, universities may be moving in a direction that could some day approach the goal of information literacy.

To identify problems unique to large universities, I interviewed library personnel at Ohio State University, the University of Michigan, the University of Illinois at Urbana, the State University of New York at Buffalo, Northwestern University, Arizona State University, the University of Washington, Cornell University, and Brigham Young University. Several problems, common to most large universities, emerged.

Size of Student Body. Many of these universities considered the size of their student bodies a limitation in developing an information literacy program. Most were successful in building instructional programs for lower-division students but were less successful in reaching upper-division and graduate students. Arizona State successfully provides an initial level of information literacy for six thousand freshmen each year; Ohio State reaches thirty thousand undergraduates; the University of Illinois at Urbana reaches twenty-five thousand undergraduates; and the University of Michigan in providing ten to twelve information literacy classes a week on a first-come, first-served basis, reaches about three thousand students a year.

Insufficient Staff. Although librarians hope to reach out to every academic discipline, and some are approaching that goal, most simply run out of staff. It is difficult in large universities to reach all students, and even more difficult to coordinate a student's work from one class to another and from year to year. If librarians are expected to provide all of the instruction for information literacy, exhaustion and failure are guaranteed.

Coordination Among Different Libraries. Ten to twenty libraries at a university may be doing library instruction independently, with no administrative coordination. Each of Ohio State's twenty-four departmental libraries has its own library instruction program. Contacts with thirty-five hundred faculty can become complicated. Academic faculty are usually independent in what they teach, resulting in information literacy programs that are designed on an ad hoc basis and thus fail to reach all students in need of the instruction. Some universities, such as the University of Washington, do not have university core courses that would provide the bases for information literacy programs.

Solutions and Successes

Many large universities are successful in overcoming these challenges. The methods vary according to university structure, curriculum requirements, and student needs. Yet some common principles apply across most programs. Most university programs are built from the bottom up. The development of sound programs, over many years, yields impressive results.

Relationships and Team Development. A team approach to developing an effective information literacy program is essential between faculty and librarians, between faculty and academic administrators, and between academic administrators and librarians. Instructional programs begin with a few faculty and librarians who see the benefits of working together. As they establish proven programs, colleagues become interested. If team development continues, not only do programs grow but campuswide support also grows. At Brigham Young University, the English Department budgeted its own funds to hire graduate assistants so that ninety-five sections of freshman English could include a research strategy unit in the curriculum. English composition administrators and faculty feel ownership for this program. They helped set the goals and define the curriculum, and they team-teach the research unit with librarians. The English Department was happy to help fund this information literacy activity because they believe in its importance for students. In time, one of the supportive English Department faculty members at Brigham Young became a dean, and another the head of the Honors Program. In these new positions, they strengthened support for information literacy programs at Brigham Young. The Honors Program subsequently invited librarians to help develop a course for all honors students. That kind of support helped not only to expand information literacy offerings but also to encourage the sharing of funds for instructional facilities and personnel.

Cooperation Across the Campus. Success across the campus depends in part on the level of centralization of university services and curriculum offerings. Information literacy can be integrated across the curriculum if it is clear who the key people are and if deans and administrators share common goals for the university. Common goals are a necessary prerequisite for developing cooperation across the campus. It is also helpful if administrators appoint library instruction committees with the responsibility to coordinate the many branch libraries that provide individual information literacy programs.

Identifying Core Courses. Many universities have worked through writing courses to reach university students. This strategy has been very successful for some universities at the lower-division levels of the curriculum with English and freshman writing classes. Other universities work with core courses in the social sciences and humanities. The University of Illinois at Urbana involves students in information literacy activities in ten different courses required for general education. The University of Washington, which requires no core classes for all students, focuses on courses that meet the university's writing requirement.

Sound Instructional Procedures. Successful information literacy programs begin with the assessment of student, department, library, and university needs and the development of goals and strategies to meet those needs. Instruction is frequently offered at different levels and in a variety of formats appropriate to the current information needs of students. The methods of instruction, such as lecture, textbook, and videotape, are selected after formulation of goals and assessments (Brottman and Loe, 1990).

Because universities have different needs, there is a great variety of program offerings. The following are some of the ways that different universities are attempting to meet their needs.

Taped Tours. The University of Illinois at Urbana and Brigham Young University have taped library tours.

Textbooks. The University of Illinois also uses a textbook in ten different courses. The text covers not only how to find information but also how to evaluate and apply it. Ohio State University uses a self-paced workbook with library assignments for incoming freshmen English students. Brigham

Young University has programmed self-instructional texts for freshman English that cover the card and on-line catalog and periodical indexes.

Courses Related and Integrated. The University of Michigan Library works with the university essay writing courses; the State University of New York at Buffalo Library works with the world civilization courses; and most universities provide course-related instruction for their academic departments. Course-integrated instruction is less common. The extension of information literacy to evaluation and application of information is a project currently receiving attention at most universities.

Videotape Presentations. Ohio State developed *Battle of the Library Superstars,* which features professional media techniques that sell students on the library as a vital part of the university (Segal, 1983). Brigham Young produced a videotape that illustrates research strategies. The video is presented in a library classroom setting, with several breakaways to illustrate concepts in a combination video-workshop format (French and Butler, 1988).

Credit Courses. Arizona State University has an optional credit course whose objective is to teach information literacy on global awareness, history awareness, cultural diversity awareness, and writing literacy. The university plans to expand the course.

Workshops. The University of Washington conducts literacy training in the university writing program. Students are divided into three groups. Group 1 identifies the underlying expertise of a work through indexes and on-line catalogs. Group 2 discerns the discourse, or what is being said in the discipline. Group 3 examines the quality of the argument of a particular work. The three groups get together and report their learning. The University of Illinois addresses the special needs of international students through specially designed workshops. Ohio State's Health Science Library holds twelve two-hour graduate research workshops a year, serving twenty to fifty students. These workshops also include a critical thinking component (Bradigan, Kroll, and Sims, 1987). Arizona State University has optional survival courses recommended for students at risk, graduate orientation laboratories, and workshops for new faculty, special needs students, and "orphan groups" (students who have no subject specialist to help them).

Tutorial Assistance. The University of Michigan offers one-on-one term paper assistance, thirty minutes per student for 100 to 150 students a year (Bergen and MacAdam, 1985). Brigham Young University offers optional workshops for library staff, faculty, and students wanting hands-on instruction on various computer systems. These optional workshops help fill a gap for individuals who want more intense training on a particular system.

Computer-Assisted Instruction Programs. Ohio State University is developing a unique user-independent computer-assisted instruction program called Gateway, designed to reach large numbers of students and to respond to their information needs. It includes, on line, thirty-one dictionaries, five general and eighty-two subject encyclopedias, seventy periodical indexes, twenty-eight biographic sources, thirty-five book review indexes, and three general and twelve specialized statistical sources. The descriptive information includes title, call number, year, brief content summary, and campus sites with current subscriptions. Local facilities are identified by name, location on map, floor plan, and collection profile. This five-year hypercard development is designed to be accessed eventually from every public terminal (Tiefel, 1991).

Another hypercard program, at the University of Maryland at College Park, introduces periodical indexes and periodical locations in the library. The program is designed to be used in classes and to stand on its own as a self-paced module, freeing instructors to use their class time for more advanced library research topics.

Resources

Information literacy programs need human, technical, and financial resources to be successful. Many universities use academic faculty and employ graduate students to assist in conducting information literacy programs. Some academic departments also provide financial support for this service.

Ohio State University secured four grants to develop its Gateway program. Cornell University and Northwestern University received grants from the Council on Library Resources to fund their information literacy programs. Brigham Young University obtained a Title II Research and Demonstration Grant to support its initiatives. These grants usually follow evidence of a strong existing program and the ability to develop an innovative improvement with potential transferability to other institutions.

Information Literacy at Brigham Young University

Brigham Young University's information literacy program illustrates how one university has dealt with the special challenges posed at large institutions. Its program has grown to the point that librarians offered over one thousand specific classes in information literacy in 1990-1991, reaching a total of 19,270 students. Much of the instruction was developed by teams of faculty and librarians. Twenty subject specialist librarians are involved in library instruction, and librarians report their progress in biannual evaluations. Nearly 100 percent of the freshman and sophomore students receive an introduction to basic skills and research strategies. More than half of the upper-division students also receive instruction on conducting research in their major fields.

The facilities to support this program include a fifty-seat training room, a rear-projection screen, and fifteen computer terminals. Instruction emphasizes research strategies, with computer applications integrated. The library and university administration are enthusiastic supporters of these instructional activities. With university administration support, presentations were given during the opening faculty conference in 1991 to deans and department chairs. Similar presentations were subsequently scheduled throughout the year for faculty in every academic department. A new library addition currently being planned will include a large auditorium and three "technology-enhanced learning environment" rooms, all connected for hands-on instruction to maximize teaching effectiveness.

The present level of sophistication is the result of more than forty years of library instruction efforts. The challenges confronting most large universities were faced by Brigham Young with its nearly twenty-eight thousand students. Library instruction began from the bottom up. In the 1940s, the English Department wanted students to find better materials on which to base the writing of their research papers. In 1970, librarians, English faculty, instructional psychology, and nonprint media specialists combined efforts to design five library instructional programs for the lower-division students.

Several goals were selected. Instruction would be designed and implemented to meet the immediate needs of students. Basic library and information skills and basic research strategies would be provided to the lower-division students; discipline-specific instruction would be provided to juniors and seniors in their major fields; and tutorial assistance would be given to graduate students and faculty. Instruction was to be provided as much as possible within the library building.

Because of the large number of students (fifty-five hundred freshmen a year) and the few librarians, basic skills instruction was developed in self-instructional packages. These included a taped tour and programmed instruction texts for card catalogs, the library's on-line catalog, and periodical indexes. Since the English composition faculty and the general education office were involved in the planning and pilot-testing of the information literacy program, it met both the curriculum needs and expectations of faculty. The English composition faculty claimed joint ownership with librarians and supervised the program. This ownership also led to substantial funding from the English Department and general education budgets to support the implementation of the program.

English faculty and librarians subsequently developed an instructional design in which English composition instructors and librarians would team-teach research strategies supported by a videotape presentation and the working through of research strategies for a specific topic. Each student follows the strategies in researching one among one hundred topics available and writing a pro-con background study paper for class. The program was developed and successfully pilot-tested with six sections of English. This resulted in the English Department wanting to expand the information literacy project to all ninety-five sections offered each semester. It again provided funding for library graduate assistants to participate. Concurrently, twenty-five subject specialist librarians joined with faculty to offer instruction to classes in their respective academic disciplines.

In 1985, the Graduate Council of the university, in evaluating the library, concluded that librarians should spend their time developing collections, and instructional endeavors relating to information literacy should be left to the teaching faculty. Because the successful information literacy program had been jointly developed and implemented by librarians and faculty, the faculty insisted that not only was the program vital to the curriculum but the librarians also were needed as part of the instructional team. As a result of this dialogue, the program's value was validated, and the partnership between faculty and librarians was better understood. The Faculty Advisory Committee subsequently recommended that the information literacy program be expanded into every academic department.

After Brigham Young University faculty and librarians attended a course-integrated bibliographic instruction workshop conducted by Earlham College librarians and faculty, the university expanded its information literacy program to the junior and senior levels of instruction by developing course-related modules designed to meet specific objectives identified by faculty in various academic programs. Initially, all subject librarians worked with any instructor who was interested, but demand often exceeded available staff time. As a partial response to this problem, efforts were made to channel instruction into research methods courses. It was generally recognized that the Brigham Young University had not yet met its goal of having a quality information literacy program in each of its academic departments and that creative solutions and alternatives were needed.

In December 1989, Brigham Young University Library was awarded a federal Title II Research and Demonstration Grant to develop and test hands-on instruction for ERIC and the library's on-line catalog in a fully equipped training center. This grant provided funding to build and equip the center with fifteen computer terminals, a rear-projection screen, and a local area network. Within one semester, demand was such that a second room was created for the video projection needs of the lower-division program. The success of activities relating to this grant increased campus-wide support for expansion of the program. In planning for a new library addition, there was strong university administrative support to provide sufficient facilities and equipment to teach students from every academic department and to provide hands-on workshops for faculty, staff, and students on specialized library resources and services.

What factors permitted an institution as large as Brigham Young University to make this progress? From the beginning of its information literacy program, the task of building relationships was very important. Quality instructional programs were developed with faculty and librarians as parts of a working team. Academic departments identified what would be helpful to their programs and their students, and the faculty became actively involved in the implementation of the program. Time was also an important factor. Even Earlham College needed to work six to seven years to reach most of its academic departments. Large universities obviously require a greater amount of time to successfully implement an information literacy program, but they can begin with one college and let the growth take care of itself. Time and quality usually combine to bring about administrative support and steady growth toward long-range goals.

Conclusion

Are large universities limited by their size in setting program goals? The answer is both yes and no! The limitations are certainly there, but at the same time a variety of large universities have successfully helped students to develop information literacy. Although no large university has yet developed a program to reach all of its students, significant progress is being made at the college and department levels. Other large universities need to examine these successful models in order to help their students achieve information literacy.

References

Bergen, K., and MacAdam, B. "One-on-One Term Paper Assistance Programs." *RQ*, 1985, *24* (3), 333-340.

Bradigan, P., Kroll, S., and Sims, S. "Graduate Student Bibliographic Instruction at a Large University: A Workshop Approach." *RQ*, 1987, *26* (3), 335-340.

Brottman, M., and Loe, M. *The LIRT Library Instruction Handbook*. Englewood, Colo.: Libraries Unlimited, 1990.

Farber, E. "Alternatives to the Term Paper." In T. G. Kirk (ed.), *Increasing the Teaching Role of Academic Libraries*. New Directions for Teaching and Learning, no. 18. San Francisco: Jossey-Bass, 1984.

French, N., and Butler, H. J. "Quiet on the Set." *Wilson Library Bulletin*, 1988, *63* (4), 42-44.

Segal, J. "*Battle of the Library Superstars:* The Use of Professional Media Production Techniques." *Library Journal*, 1983, *108* (8), 795-797.

Tiefel, V. "The Gateway to Information: A System Redefines How Libraries Are Used." *American Libraries*, 1991, *22* (9), 558-560.

MARVIN E. WIGGINS is behavioral science librarian and chair of the Department of Social Sciences of the Harold B. Lee Library at Brigham Young University, Provo, Utah.

The ultimate goal is to have faculty fully incorporate an information literacy component into the curriculum.

Expository Writing and Information Literacy: A Pilot Project

Marianne I. Gaunt, Stan Nash

For many years, the Rutgers University libraries have conducted an active bibliographic instruction program typical of most university libraries: orientations for new students, special programs and term paper clinics, individual library class instruction at the request of teaching faculty, and credit courses in library research strategies. A small program to instruct teaching assistants on incorporating library skills into their classes was a first effort at instructor-directed information literacy. While these approaches have been favorably received by the teaching faculty, they do not provide the opportunity to reinforce a progression of information skills throughout the duration of a course. Librarians were seeking ways to revamp the program to provide a more comprehensive and effective approach to information literacy but had not been successful in finding an appropriate entry point for a campuswide discussion with teaching faculty. Then, in early 1991, an opportunity arose.

Background

In early 1990, the provost of the New Brunswick campus of Rutgers University appointed a committee to make recommendations on ways to improve undergraduate education. When the committee's report was distributed for campus review and response, the library faculty remarked on the absence of any reference to the role played by the library in the undergraduate experience. The vice president for university libraries asked a small library committee to prepare a written response to the report, focusing on the educational role of the library and including concrete recommendations in the area of information literacy.

The library's response was brief and focused on the importance of information literacy not only for a successful undergraduate experience but for lifelong learning. The library faculty listed the characteristics of an information literate person in terms of information-seeking skills in the college environment and suggested at least five ways in which the library could assist the teaching faculty in ensuring that all Rutgers students would achieve these skills before graduation. Regardless of the methodology chosen, both the teaching faculty and librarians would need to assess the impact of these recommendations on the human resources required to carry them out effectively.

The provost referred the library's response to his Faculty Council Committee on the Library in advance of a full hearing before the entire Faculty Council. This committee embraced the notion that information literacy was important for all students and suggested a pilot program within a few freshmen English classes to test a methodology. English 102 was chosen for the pilot because it is required of nearly half our undergraduates, it seeks to develop critical thinking skills, assignments include the writing of a short research essay, and it has historically included a library component. The committee's recommendations were endorsed by the entire Faculty Council and an implementation committee was formed. This group was composed of the associate university librarian for research and undergraduate services, the director of the Writing Program, and the bibliographic instruction coordinators of the four major Rutgers libraries in New Brunswick. This committee was to design the pilot program, select the participating teaching faculty and librarians, prepare an evaluation and assessment of the pilot, and make recommendations for changes and/or expansion. The pilot program began during the fall 1991 semester.

Goals of the Project

The ultimate goal is to have the faculty fully incorporate an information literacy component into the curriculum. This can be achieved only if teaching faculty substantially alter the manner in which they currently teach their courses. Until that change happens, librarians must be content with the progress made to date: campuswide discussion and acceptance of information literacy as an important component of undergraduate education and a validation of the librarian's role in enhancing the undergraduate experience. When the assessment of the current pilot project is completed, we expect to move forward toward the next stage of working closely with the teaching faculty to develop a more fully integrated program.

Implementing the Pilot Project

Six department faculty who teach sections of English 102 agreed to participate in the pilot project. Librarians were invited to give two library research seminars designed to meet information needs of students at two given points in the semester and in the process establish a foundation for achieving information literacy. The following procedures acted as guidelines for the four librarians who taught these sessions. While some variations were introduced by individual librarians, all followed essentially the same procedures. The overall design included a judicious deployment of a combination of hands-on experience, lecture, discussion, and written materials, presented at the juncture when the students had very specific information needs.

Research Seminar 1: Fourth Class Meeting. The course assignment at this time requires students to find periodical articles and/or books on a subject of their choice. At this time, each of the librarians participating in the pilot conducts a seminar for the classes to which he or she is assigned. The purpose of this first seminar is to introduce students to the basic mechanics of using the library and the basic concepts of library research, with an emphasis on periodical literature and indexes.

As part of the session, students are required to do a library assignment. This assignment is completed and evaluated during class time. Approximately forty minutes are devoted to the class presentation and forty to the assignments and an evaluation of the results. Coverage includes the following tools and concepts: (1) The value of seeking assistance from reference librarians is discussed. (2) An in-depth discussion of the nature of periodicals (scholarly versus trade and popular, political biases, and other features), the variations in periodical indexes, and the use of compact disk-read only memory (CD-ROM) indexes is conducted. Also included is information on locating periodicals in the library, materials delivery (campus-to-campus delivery of books and articles), and interlibrary loan. (3) *Info Trac* is used to illustrate several important concepts and to emphasize the importance of exercising critical judgment in choosing an information source through careful examination of the information given in citations, such as the title of the periodical, the length of the articles, and the type of article (for example, book review). Librarians also stress the various access points by which one may search, including principles of Boolean logic. (4) There is a brief discussion of other periodical indexes, both in paper and in CD-ROM format, stressing the *Social Sciences Index* and *Humanities Index*. The *Public Affairs Information Service Bulletin* is introduced as a good starting point for government information. And (5) there is an in-depth discussion of Rutgers University libraries' on-line catalog and its relationship to the card catalog. This discussion includes an introduction to the *Library of Congress Subject Headings* and keyword and Boolean searching on the on-line catalog. Librarians briefly review the Library of Congress classification scheme and strategies for locating books in the library.

The assignment consists of having students search the topics that they are working on both in the on-line catalog and in *Info Trac*. For the on-line catalog, students have to first determine the Library of Congress subject headings for their respective subjects and then do both a subject search and keyword search, noting the difference in the number of items retrieved. For *Info Trac,* the students have to print out lists of items retrieved on their subjects and analyze the articles found with regard to the nature of the periodicals (scholarly, trade, or popular), the length of the articles, and anything unusual that they noticed about the documents on their respective lists. For any one of the items found, they also have to determine if it is owned by the Rutgers library system and, if so, precisely where they can find it. To avoid undue competition for library resources, each class is divided into four teams. Each team has to do the whole assignment together; they are not allowed to divide up the work. While one team member searches, the other team members observe and add their input, advice, and coaching. The English instructors have the option of forming the teams around a common theme or themes related to the class readings. Both the faculty member and the librarian are available to give help and advice to the teams as they work through this assignment.

To fill in gaps and to address those learning styles that favor written materials, each student is given several handouts to accompany the class presentation. One of these handouts is a pathfinder, listing the most essential reference tools, including periodical indexes, appropriate to the general category of each class. These handouts are meant to instill in students the concept of using a research strategy and are designed as beginning guides for their research for a ten-page essay that begins about the eighth week of this course. The students also receive guides to the particular Rutgers libraries that they are using for the class, which describe the key locations and services at those libraries. Librarians also have the option of giving out other handouts, either on their own initiative or at the request of the faculty members. For example, some choose to give out guides on such topics as research strategy and plagiarism.

Research Seminar 2: Eighth Week of the Course. By the eighth week of the English 102 course, students have written proposals for ten-page research essays. Each librarian participating in the project has had an advance look at the specific topics that the students have chosen. In Seminar 2, the librarian, the faculty member, and the students discuss problems that students are having with their research. The librarians make specific suggestions on how to overcome these problems or to find additional information. During these sessions, the librarians strive to reinforce lessons on information literacy as they relate to the ensuing discussion. The following concepts are considered to have the highest priority: (1) range of paper and computerized periodical indexes; (2) evaluation of the quality and relevance of sources, including biases inherent to periodicals and reference sources (for example, the government-issued *Encyclopedia of South Africa*) and ways of assessing alternative points of view (for example, using tools such as the *Alternative Press Index*); (3) access points, that is, keyword versus subject searching with controlled vocabulary; (4) importance and usefulness of bibliographies; (5) purpose and range of reference works, including finding discrete information quickly (for example, statistics and definitions), getting background on a topic, and locating sources outside the library; (6) ways of focusing on a topic (for example, by discipline or time frame); and (7) development of a research strategy.

Assessing the Pilot Project

Librarians and faculty members devised several assessment tools to determine the pilot project's effectiveness and to discover ways of improving and refining the larger program anticipated to result from this project. The assessment process included gathering feedback from the students, the English Department faculty, and the librarians directly involved with the pilot test.

Students completed questionnaires after each of the two library research seminars. The questionnaire used for the first session includes two questions asking the students to identify the most and least helpful "things" about that session, and a list of library tools or processes on which to indicate whether we should have provided more or less coverage. For the second session, we simply asked the students to write two paragraphs in completing the following sentences: "The way(s) in which this class was helpful to me . . . " and "The trouble with this class was. . . ."

Of the 121 students who returned questionnaires from the first session, the clearest message came from the 61 percent who considered the hands-on experience with various library computing systems to be the most valuable part of the class. No other item came even close to being listed so many times in reply to that query. Conversely, among the relatively few responses to the question concerning the least helpful aspect of the session, the library lecture was listed more times than any other aspect. Regarding the process and tools covered in this first session, the desire for more coverage of computerized information sources and less coverage of the card catalog stood out the most prominently. Forty percent of the students expressed a desire for more coverage of the on-line catalog, while 12 percent thought we should have given it less time. Fifty percent of the students wanted more time on *Info Trac* and CD-ROM periodical indexes. Surprising to us, 41 percent of the students indicated that more attention should be given to the process of finding books, and 29 percent wanted more attention given to the Library of Congress classification scheme! These latter two percentages seemed high to us since there was much probing during the classroom presentations to ferret out problems students might be having in these areas. The responses convinced us that coverage of library basics is very much in order, given that 59 percent of these students were sophomores and 31 percent were juniors.

Two strong messages came through from the student responses to the second library research seminar. First, while many thought that the best part of this process is the attention paid to their individual topics, a number of students were "bored" listening to the discussions of other students' topics. Although the percentages of bored students varied from class to class, this sentiment was expressed frequently enough for us to reconsider our original premise that students would enthusiastically learn from discussions of their fellow students' research problems and from the various solutions provided by the librarians and course instructors. Second, many students wanted less discussion of and more hands-on experience with or demonstrations of how to use computers and reference tools. Thus, modification of the second seminar is in order. Several librarians and English 102 instructors have suggested running the second session more like a term paper clinic, with some discussion afterward, summing up valuable lessons learned that would be applicable to all students. This approach might be a more effective use of the seminar time than is joint discussion of the research needs of all students.

Several other key assessment tools are the observations of librarians and course instructors throughout the project; the responses of the course instructors to a detailed questionnaire on the quality of the sources that students used in writing their research essays; and analyses of the final papers by the librarians who instructed the students. Based on discussions between the project coordinator, the librarians, and the course instructors involved, it seems evident that students learn more from the library research seminars than they do from the single library lecture. Moreover, students are more receptive to library instruction that is given in a timely fashion and that addresses their actual information needs. One English 102 faculty member, who had previously participated in numerous library instruction sessions, commented that the first session was the best research seminar that she had ever experienced. From her perspective, the students were enthusiastic and attentive and had learned a great deal about information seeking. Nearly all of the course instructors and librarians felt that the hands-on approach makes library learning more palatable and meaningful and thus is a far more effective method of teaching in comparison to lecturing. The interaction between the course instructor, librarians, and students during the first session provided many opportunities for reinforcing the students' understanding of such things as the nature of periodicals, periodical indexes, and controlled vocabulary searching. The main problem perceived was time pressure—all participants felt rushed, and the librarians wondered if they had really adequately covered every topic. However, most of the librarians and all of the English 102 faculty felt that the quality of learning achieved is more important than the quantity of material presented.

The main deficiency of the second seminar is the lack of cogency, partly due to the absence of any direct or hands-on experience with the reference tools being discussed. It was originally thought that by the time of the second seminar, most of the students would have completed sufficient work on their respective topics to generate many questions regarding library research. In fact, it took great effort to coax students into discussing their topics. Moreover, many seemed shy about admitting that they had problems with research. Yet, after the session, many approached the librarians with a host of questions that would have been very useful for class discussion. It should be stressed, however, that although students derived much benefit from both library research seminars, they did not learn as much as we had expected in the second semester.

Based on comments from the librarians, the key factor for success in the second session was the constructive involvement of the course instructors. Their ability to draw out students and their personal knowledge of the library and the research problems associated with students' topics were crucial in starting meaningful discussions and in sustaining those dialogues. Indeed, this pilot program, because it is so dependent on a good working relationship between librarians and English 102 instructors, serves to foster the coveted "partnership" between faculty and librarian that so many librarians allude to in library literature.

In responding to the questionnaire about the sources that students used in their research essays, the English 102 instructors' evaluations were very positive on the whole. To the lead and perhaps most important question of whether these students in the pilot project used better quality sources than did previous students in the course, four of the six instructors answered yes. The fifth instructor felt that students were not using enough scholarly materials. And the sixth maintained that there was no substantial difference between the quality of sources used in the second semester compared to previous classes. However, he qualified this assessment by stating that "what is significantly different is the use of sources by weak students." Many of these students, whom he characterized as "C+ students," became B students "in large part" because of the quality of the sources that they employed in their research essays. This evaluation was indeed gratifying to read, since it is average students who are in most need of help from librarians.

There is much variation in the responses to the other questions asked of the English 102 instructors. Many of these replies identify areas that require greater emphasis if students are to achieve information literacy. In answer to a series of questions about the level of critical judgment shown by students in selecting and utilizing information sources, the instructors revealed that in two-thirds of the classes many students were not sufficiently aware of the biases of the authors to whom they referred. Moreover, in all of the classes many students, often the majority, failed to express more than one point-of-view on their topics. But they did well in selecting appropriate and timely sources. Overall, it is evident from this assessment that more emphasis needs to be placed on critical thinking in library instruction.

The English 102 instructors were also asked to comment on the effectiveness of the method used in this pilot project. All agreed that both library sessions were valuable. The first seminar received very high praise; however, several instructors thought that the second seminar was more valuable because it was given when students were working on library-oriented research assignments. Consistent with earlier observations, several instructors felt that the second seminar did not garner enough involvement from the students. After their individual topics were addressed, students did not show interest in drawing meaningful lessons from the research problems of other students. For example, one instructor wrote, "Some students seemed to 'tune out' when the spotlight moved on to someone else." Yet, in several cases, the second seminar was considered the best part of the pilot and students were in fact seen as very involved in the discussion. Given the students' reactions and other observations from both librarians and instructors participating in the pilot, the second seminar was modified to be more adaptable to students' different learning styles and instructors' different teaching styles.

With respect to the human resources necessary to continue an information literacy program of this kind, we have decided to continue refining the pilot until we feel that we have a program that satisfies all participants and is more "marketable" to other faculty. During this adjustment phase, we may devolve some of the teaching directly to the faculty who have participated in several sessions and, at the same time, develop a more tightly packaged instructional program for the librarians involved.

Conclusion

Much has been accomplished at Rutgers University in developing an information literacy program; much more remains to be done. We are learning from our pilot test and are prepared to make changes to strengthen the program. But the basic strategy of integrating library research seminars into a course when student information needs are strongest, combined with a mixture of discussion and hands-on teaching, is a highly effective method of providing a strong foundation for information literacy in undergraduate education.

MARIANNE I. GAUNT *is associate university librarian for research and undergraduate services at Rutgers University, New Brunswick, New Jersey.*

STAN NASH *is bibliographic instruction coordinator for the Archibald Stevens Alexander Library, the main research library for the social sciences and humanities at Rutgers University.*

Our current notion of literacy, including the skills that we associate with it, has evolved from the technology of the quill pen, paper, movable type, and mechanically powered rotary press to the new electronic technology.

The Electronic Library and Literacy

Jan Kennedy Olsen

Librarians' traditional theories and practices have provided society with access to the world's information. Access, however, was based in the print format. Today, information is generated in electronic form, and the nation's librarians are facing the challenge of implementing the electronic library. In this chapter, I describe the electronic library and Cornell University's efforts to prepare students to use it.

The Electronic Library

The vision of the electronic library is centered on the user at the workstation. The *workstation* is defined as each user's microcomputer connected to a local network, which is connected to state, regional, national, and international networks. Users enter the electronic library through a single window or "gateway." The locus for users' access to information is now outside the library's four walls; it has become the home, the office, or the laboratory.

The electronic library can be conceptualized in terms of broad categories or types of information. The first is bibliographic information. Bibliographic data bases provide users with citations to the literature of a discipline. Examples of these on-line sources are MEDLINE, *Chemical Abstracts*, and ERIC. The holdings of a library collection, or, at a wider level, the holdings of many libraries, constitute another form of bibliographic data bases. The second category of information is the full text of documents. Ideally, in an electronic library, users can search a bibliographic data base such as MEDLINE, or a library's holdings, and generate a list of citations. Each citation would then be linked to the full text, which would be retrieved and displayed on the screen. The third category of information is numerical data, such as U.S. Census data. Here, typically, users will want to extract a subset of data related to a topic and will also want to be able to identify all other numerical files that contain related data. The fourth category is a combination of numerical and textual data, such as the Genbank data base. This data base is a record of all reported nucleic acid sequences and is used by scholars working on DNA sequences as a means of checking whether or not the particular sequence with which they are working has already been identified. There are other broad categories of information that in time will also become part of the electronic library, such as spatial data, images, and sounds.

The electronic library's resources can be stored at the user's local level, loaded on a machine within the user's institution. National data bases may be mounted locally and accessed by the local community under a license agreement. In addition, the electronic library provides access to resources that are stored at a remote location and are available via government networks, private networks, and national and international networks. The locations of resources will not be of any concern to users, and the modes of access will be transparent.

This scenario of users at workstations accessing data and the full texts of literature, regardless of the locations of the users or of the information, depicts the current challenge to librarians, who need to create a new paradigm for providing access to information in the electronic library. They need to ensure that a wide variety of information resources are accessible, that this accessibility is presented to the users in an intelligible way, that the data resources are usable, that the workstations can perform the functions well, and that the telecommunications systems have sufficient bandwidth to support the sharing of information resources among institutions.

The Electronic Library and Literacy

As we move through the twenty-first century, the electronic library will increasingly displace the print library as the primary means of storing and accessing the world's information. To be able to exploit this electronic information, individuals will have to acquire a new set of information skills. They will have to expand the traditional skills of literacy.

Hunter and Harman (1985, pp. 7-8) define literacy as

> the possession of skills perceived as necessary by particular persons and groups to fulfill their own self-determined objectives as family and community members, citizens, consumers, job-holders and members of social, religious or other associations of their choosing. This includes the ability to obtain information they want and to use the information for their own and others' well being; the ability to read and write adequately to

satisfy the requirements they set for themselves as being important for their own lives, the ability to deal positively with demands made on them by society and the ability to solve the problems they face in their daily lives.

The entry-level skills of literacy, as we know it today, are the abilities to read and write. However, in the West, before the written record came into widespread use in eleventh-century England, the oral tradition dominated. To be literate meant the ability to compose and recite orally. The spoken word was the legally valid record.

With the emergence of the quill pen and the production of written texts on paper, the world saw the first technologies that eventually brought us to our current concept of functional literacy. The steam-driven rotary press and innovations in the manufacturing of paper have also played a significant role in developing the skills of literacy that allow the masses to use the information needed to function in society. The current notion of literacy has evolved from the technology of the quill pen, paper, movable type, and mechanically powered rotary press. The skills that we call literacy have evolved with technology.

Today, the dominant technologies are computers and telecommunications. In their turn, they too are forcing a fundamental innovation in the nature of information and how it is used by society. As today's technologies force the transition from information in print to information in electronic form, the skills of reading and writing are no longer sufficient for literacy. To them we must add new skills for obtaining and using information from a variety of electronic systems and formats. The traditional notion of literacy must expand to include skills of information literacy. Literacy no longer means the ability to read, write, and complete basic mathematical operations. The demands of an information-and-service-based economy require the development of these skills at a more advanced level than that needed in an industrial-based economy (Blake and Tjoumas, 1990).

Information Literacy Education

MacDonald (1966) asked whether it is the library's job to teach and concluded that the library's job is to see that teaching gets done. In university and college environments, the question and answer are pertinent. Libraries have a responsibility to see that their resources are used. And, traditionally, the librarians have instructed students in the use of bibliographic tools. As these tools have become computerized, librarians have moved into teaching users how to work with electronic versions.

This traditional instruction, however, does not acknowledge the basic principle at issue today. Computer technology is forcing a fundamental innovation in the way that information is conceptualized, stored, accessed, and used. As the electronic library emerges, the traditional literacy skills of reading and writing will no longer be sufficient for effective use of this new form of the library. Colleges and universities must produce students who are information literate in an electronic world.

Today, there is extensive concern about the state of students' literacy. But there is little, if any, discussion of the implications of the computer age for traditional literacy, and the responsibility of undergraduate education to respond to the new standards of literacy. In the report *A Nation at Risk: The Imperative for Educational Reform*, the U.S. National Commission on Excellence in Education (1983) recognized that effective participation in our "learning society" requires each person to be able to manage complex information in electronic and digital form and, therefore, placed great importance on computer literacy. As Compaine (1984) asserts, however, computer literacy is not enough. He presents the possibility that a "new literacy" might indeed evolve as the result of the Information Age. But this type of literacy is not enough either. The skills of information literacy essential to effective functioning in today's society must be cognitively developed in as fundamental a way as the skills of reading and writing.

A review of national activity in the area of information literacy makes clear that there is considerable variation and vagueness in the meaning of the term. This vagueness of definition creates confusion not only in what information literacy means but also in what must be taught to develop it in an individual. In practical terms, graduates who are information literate will, in addition to the traditional skills of literacy, understand the role, power, and uses of information; understand the variety of contents and formats of information; understand systems for organizing information; have the capability to retrieve information; and have the ability to evaluate, organize, and manipulate information.

Information Literacy Education at Mann Library

An information literacy instruction program has been in existence at Cornell University's Mann Library since 1986. The program formally began when a job was posted for a coordinator of information literacy. The information literacy program provides an explicit curriculum designed to develop information literacy in undergraduates through the teaching of information management skills. The teaching of these skills is enhanced by Mann's electronic library, which serves as a teaching "laboratory." Students have access to resources in the electronic library through a computer interface accessible from microcomputer centers on campus and from individuals' workstations.

Mann Library provides instruction to a population of over 5,000 undergraduates, approximately 1,500 graduate students, and 650 faculty in the College of Agriculture and Life Sciences, College of Human Ecology, and

Division of Biological Sciences. The two primary teaching strategies are course-related instruction and a series of workshops.

In course-related instruction, librarians teach information management skills related to specific coursework and assignments. Instruction is usually provided at faculty request and takes place during regular class sessions or in separately scheduled sessions. This instruction is very popular. Most students receiving this instruction believe that their abilities to complete class assignments will improve as they acquire information management skills. Students have immediate opportunities to put what they learn into practice. Course-related instruction also allows librarians, students, and faculty to form valuable collegial ties in their work together.

Mann's workshop series are also very popular. Workshops in word processing, spreadsheets, bibliographic searching, and file management are provided. The workshops are voluntary and are typically attended by people who have an immediate need to use a system or software package. Multiple sessions of each workshop are offered every semester to provide students with ample opportunities to receive instruction. The workshops consist of lectures, demonstrations, and hands-on practice. These are supplemented by an individual tutorial for each workshop participant. Recent studies by Cornell librarians clearly show the need for this individualized instruction (Stewart and Olsen, 1988; Spragg, 1990) and the importance of reinforcing instruction with hands-on system practice (Stewart, 1990).

However, the combined strategies of course-related instruction and workshops, while reaching thousands of students over the years, have serious shortcomings.

Instruction Fails to Cover the Full Range of Information Management Skills. Course-related instruction is limited to support of the subject at hand. Instructors must begin with the basics in every class session since students rarely come to the class with basic knowledge and skills. As a result, students often hear the same lecture material repeated in different classes where librarians are invited to lecture rather than presentations of more advanced material.

Workshops are strictly oriented toward practical skills. They include information on organizational concepts but are primarily training sessions in particular systems. They fail to provide a broad range of information management knowledge and skills. Even if workshops in every area are offered, very few students participate in all of them, particularly if no credit is given.

Instruction Fails to Reach All Students. Course-related instruction is presented to students in scattered subject areas. Teaching opportunities depend on the interest of faculty. Many faculty do not devote classroom time to information management skills. Workshops are available for all students to attend but are voluntary and carry no course credit. It is often quite difficult for undergraduates to find open time in their heavy class schedules. When they do have time, many are loathe to devote it to a class where no course credit is given.

Instruction Is Extremely Labor Intensive. Although thousands of undergraduates from within the primary user group receive no instruction, the library's teaching resources are completely consumed by its workshops and course-related instruction.

Lessons Learned. From our experience we have leaned the following lessons: (1) Students' motivation to learn is stimulated by course credit, course requirements, and satisfaction of immediate needs. (2) Students require hands-on experience when they are learning systems and software. (3) Course-related instruction is practical for only a very limited range of information management knowledge and skills. (4) Neither workshops nor course-related instruction reach enough students. (5) Individual tutorials affirm concepts and skills learned in a workshop session. (6) Students recognize the need for information management instruction. And (7) implementation of a cohesive curriculum that is mainstreamed into undergraduate education is very difficult because students do not necessarily take a sequence of classes in the recommended order, making incremental learning in course-related instruction impossible.

Tutorial Experiment

Mann Library has conducted several research projects in an effort to overcome some of the past shortcomings of the information literacy program. Individual tutorials are an integral part of Mann's workshop program. Students who take the workshop on bibliographic data bases later conduct their own searches with the supervision of a librarian "coach." An evaluation of the workshop's tutorial component was conducted to assess the need for this kind of labor-intensive instruction process. Tutorial sessions were tape-recorded as coaches assisted students in their searches of bibliographic data bases. Students were interviewed after the searches were completed.

Student comments showed a clear need for staff assistance during an individual's first search. Opinions differed on whether the coach should remain in the office during subsequent searches; some students would be satisfied if staff simply remained near the office, accessible for answering questions. Coaches were expected to promote confidence, clear up misunderstood concepts, provide guided practice in interacting with the system, and help ensure that searchers were satisfied with the results of their searches. Features that were explained frequently during the searches include procedures for saving and executing searches, strategies for searching the same topics on multiple data bases; interpretation of handouts and printed search aids; and use of the data base descriptions list at the reference desk.

Mere availability of systems is not enough; students need training to use them effectively. Mann's study concentrated on the BRS Menus of Bibliographic Retrieval Services, which charges for on-line time. Mann's clientele are spread over a full range of life sciences and social sciences students; and although many compact disk-read only memory (CD-ROM) data bases are offered, availability of all possible data bases through this medium would not be feasible. Moreover, thirteen of Mann's nineteen test participants had attempted CD-ROM data base searches prior to their on-line searches. At least three of these participants commented that their CD-ROM searches had not been as successful as their on-line searches. All participants required considerable assistance using BRS Menus, regardless of prior CD-ROM use. It is probable they would have benefited from additional help in using the CD-ROMs as well.

Ironically, with all of the time spent by tutors in assisting students with vocabulary and strategy construction, many students still saw search commands and manipulation of the computer as the most problematic aspects of searching. As revealed in numerous comments during the interviews about learning to use a thesaurus and think of search terms, students were appreciative of these skills and made progress in them, but the skills were not uppermost in their minds as they thought about searching.

Most students needed extensive assistance during their first search. Library staff decided to retain the coaching program and increase the amount of time scheduled for a first-time search from a half-hour to one hour. Only a half-hour, however, will actually be spent on line, which should enable coaches to explain material more comprehensively before the search so that less on-line time is used for explanations.

In addition to data bases accessed from the library, librarians are now providing data base access to users at remote locations such as their homes, offices, and dormitories. Since it is not practical to coach students through every search, the next question to address is the development of support systems for remote users. An innovative approach has been taken by one commercial vendor. The Life Science Network, sponsored by BIOSIS, offers an on-line consultant during hours of highest use.

Credit Course Experiment

In fall 1990, Mann Library offered a half-semester, two-credit class in the Communications Department. The course covered information evaluation, selection, access, retrieval, organization, storage, and communication. It was intended to overcome several past deficiencies of the instruction program by providing hands-on laboratories, a cohesive curriculum, a full range of in-depth knowledge and skills pertaining to the various information technologies central to the use of scholarly information, incremental learning, the motivation of earning credit, control of class content, and the opportunity to build rapport between students and instructors.

The syllabus indicated that students would receive hands-on instruction in the use of a variety of information systems and software and that topics to be covered included the structure of scholarly information; searches of bibliographic, numerical, and full-text data bases; use of data base, spreadsheet, and statistical software to manage information; and use of national and international networks for scholarly communication. Students who took the course would be able to understand the structure of scholarly information; evaluate the quality of information; understand the power of information in contemporary society; find and use information available at Cornell libraries and other specialized resources; understand and use telecommunications software and systems; understand definitions and uses of bibliographic, textual, and numerical data; use command languages and Boolean logic to search computerized data bases; and use microcomputer software such as data base management packages and spreadsheet packages to store and manage information (Ochs, Barnes, Coons, and Van Ostrand, 1991). Overall, the course provided students with the knowledge base and skills necessary for the effective use of libraries, print and electronic, throughout their academic careers.

Cohesive Curriculum Experiment

This instruction program was designed in cooperation with the curriculum committee of the Department of Agricultural Economics. Library staff taught information management knowledge and skills to business and finance majors.

The intent of this program is to provide a cohesive curriculum, to be taken in a sequence of classes required of freshmen, sophomores, juniors, and seniors. A complete range of information skills and knowledge is learned incrementally, each class building on the content of the previous class. Also, the program reaches a large group of students. According to the statement of goals and objectives for the program, students within the colleges and divisions served by Mann Library should possess the following core information literacy competencies after their four undergraduate years at Cornell.

Goal A. Understand the role and power of information in a democratic society. Students can describe and understand (1) how scholars, researchers, and practicing professionals use information and keep currently informed; (2) how the use of information can improve the quality of scholars' and professionals' work; (3) the commodity nature of information—who generates, controls, and uses information—and, in particular, the role that governments play in the dissemination and control of information; and (4) the costs of misinformation and the possibilities and consequences of abuse.

Goal B. Understand the variety of the content and format of information. Within their respective disciplines, students can (1) distinguish popular from scholarly treatments of a subject; (2) distinguish between primary and secondary sources; (3) define various standard formats for the storage of scholarly information, for example, print, microform, optical, floppy and compact disks, and magnetic tape; (4) evaluate the quality of information and the usefulness of the content and format of a particular information tool based on relevant criteria; and (5) identify appropriate print or computerized information resources and describe their value.

Goal C. Understand standard systems for the organization of information. Within their disciplines, students can (1) define types of data bases, their organizational structure, and the retrieval function and process; (2) recognize that different types of reference sources lead to various forms and formats of information; (3) define standard terms such as bibliographic citation, periodical index, abstract, and citation index; (4) differentiate between the types of materials typically represented in a library's catalog and those that are not; and (5) determine the index structure and access points of print and computerized information resources.

Goal D. Develop the capability to retrieve information from a variety of systems and formats. Within their disciplines, students can (1) construct logical plans to organize their searches for information; (2) describe the differences between controlled vocabularies and keywords and use both efficiently in their search strategy; (3) effectively use logical operators (and, or, not) to link their search terms and intersect concepts in various electronic information systems; (4) understand and apply the concepts of truncation and field qualification in various electronic information systems; (5) describe and use appropriate services that are available to assist them in locating information; (6) successfully navigate within libraries; (7) accurately interpret bibliographic citations from print and computerized information resources and locate the materials that they represent; and (8) operate a standard personal computer, develop mastery of certain programs and software, and maintain a working awareness of other software programs.

Goal E. Develop the ability to organize and manipulate information for various access and retrieval purposes. Within their disciplines, students can (1) use a bibliographic file management package to organize downloaded citations and personal files of references; (2) conduct their own needs assessment, based on relevant criteria, to identify suitable software packages appropriate to given applications; (3) use electronic spreadsheets to reformat and analyze numerical data that have been either downloaded or manually entered into the package; (4) use a word-processing package to format papers, reformat downloaded references, and construct bibliographies; and (5) write correct bibliographic citations.

Workplace Expectations

Mann Library received a grant from the American Library Association to assess the effectiveness of Mann's information literacy instruction program, to identify the information skills that employers would like to see in graduates, and to determine which skills the graduates themselves found necessary in their jobs (Ochs, Barnes, Coons, and Van Ostrand, 1991). Two surveys were designed and administered. The first surveyed employers of Cornell graduates, and the second surveyed recent graduates from the business and finance program within the Department of Agricultural Economics, the department where our information literacy prototype curriculum had been tested.

The questionnaire administered to employers of recent Cornell graduates was designed to determine which information skills employers consider important in recent graduates. Questions were intended to reveal how business people perceive information skills and whether there is any relationship among these perceptions based on size of business, type of industry, or profession. The population for the survey of 625 employers consisted of 284 recruiters who visited Cornell to interview potential employees, 259 alumni who graduated between 1950 and 1970 with administrative positions in business, and 82 supervisors of recent business and finance graduates.

We surveyed employers about their expectations for skills in six different areas: (1) finding information in computerized data bases, (2) manipulating numerical data with a computer, (3) creating and managing data bases, (4) writing computer programs, (5) preparing and producing documents using computers, and (6) using computer telecommunications networks and software. Employers ranked the skill levels expected in a number of specific areas within each of these broad categories of information skills. A similar methodology was followed in our survey of recent Cornell business and finance graduates. The population consisted of 599 alumni who graduated between May 1988 and May 1990. Alumni evaluated the skill levels expected of them in their new positions in the same six areas outlined above. Recent graduates also were asked to identify the methods that they used to learn these skills and to rate the importance of these methods.

The surveys provided us with an excellent perspective on the skills required of business and finance graduates, an understanding of the needs and priorities of the employers, and an overall sense of the value of the concept of information literacy as perceived by students and their employers. Results indicate that computers are used by many employees, and that information skills are considered important in the hiring process by employers. As indicated by their comments, some employers, while not already using computer technology throughout their organizations, felt that the need for computer skills in their organizations will increase over the next several years. Since we are training future leaders for industry, it is this increasing need that our programs must meet.

Numbers and statistics can tell much, but written comments have a powerful voice. We allowed space on the surveys for respondents to express their ideas on the value of information or the importance of computers in their companies or in individual jobs. One of the purposes of our study was to determine whether the managers and workers in industry today share our philosophy on the importance of information skills. This quote, from one of our survey respondents, perhaps answers that question. "In this decade we will realize there are only two options: understand information supported by computer technology and have a shot at success or ignore [its] value and assure failure."

The most important task now is to identify the surveys' implications for the definition of information literacy. The following conclusions have been drawn from the data: (1) Computer skills are considered in the hiring process and may give students an edge. However, more important, these skills are valuable to the effective performance of students' jobs once they have them. (2) Computers are used in many companies currently, and their use is increasing. (3) Few employers expect intermediate or advanced skills except when hiring for very specific positions. (4) Use of computers does not seem to vary by industry or by size of the organization. Thus, skills in managing information with computers are needed for whatever type of business-related career a person is preparing. And (5) students require less training in mainframe computer programming languages and more training in the use of applications software, including programming within these packages.

Conclusion

During the last four years, formal evaluation of the information literacy instruction program, together with experiments in different models of instruction, has increased our understanding of the concept of information literacy, the most appropriate skills and knowledge to be taught, and the class arrangements most compatible with the undergraduate's schedule. We are now in a position to synthesize the data from our investigations and to formulate the next iteration of our information literacy program.

References

Blake, V. P., and Tjoumas, R. (eds.). *Information Literacies for the Twenty-First Century*. Boston: Hall, 1990.
Compaine, B. M. *Information Technology and Cultural Change: Toward a New Literacy*. Cambridge, Mass.: Center for Information Policy Research, Harvard University, 1984.
Hunter, C., and Harman, D. *Adult Illiteracy in the United States: A Report to the Ford Foundation*. New York: McGraw-Hill, 1985.
MacDonald, B. *Literacy Activities in Public Libraries: A Report of a Study of Services to Adult Illiterates*. Chicago: American Library Association, 1966.
Ochs, M., Barnes, S., Coons, B., and Van Ostrand, D. *Assessing the Value of an Information Literacy Program*. Ithaca, N.Y.: Albert R. Mann Library, Cornell University, 1991.
Spragg, E. *CD-ROM Interface Evaluation: Comparison of Searching ERIC on IBM and Macintosh*.

Final Report to Apple Computer. Ithaca, N.Y.: Albert R. Mann Library, Cornell University, 1990.

Stewart, L. *Computerized Literature Searching: Evaluating One-on-One Interactions.* Ithaca, N.Y.: Albert R. Mann Library, Cornell University, 1990.

Stewart, L., and Olsen, J. "Compact Disk Data Bases: Are They Good for Users?" *Online,* 1988, *12* (3), 48–52.

U.S. National Commission on Excellence in Education. *A Nation at Risk: The Imperative for Educational Reform.* Washington, D.C.: Government Printing Office, 1983.

JAN KENNEDY OLSEN *is director of the Albert R. Mann Library, Cornell University, Ithaca, New York.*

Faculty, librarians, and students have yet to embrace the attitudinal change necessary for making information literacy and resource-based learning together a priority and a reality in higher education.

Information Literacy: Overcoming Barriers to Implementation

D. W. Farmer

Literacy in America can no longer be considered merely the ability to read. The Information Age requires that the concept of literacy be expanded to include information literacy—the ability to locate, evaluate, synthesize, organize, and apply information. In this Information Age, Americans must be effective information consumers in all fields of knowledge and have the capacity to make connections among a variety of information sources.

A growing awareness of the need for information literacy throughout the United States prompted the American Library Association to commission a group of educators to explore this topic. Their report noted that "to respond effectively to an ever-changing environment, people need more than just a knowledge base, they also need techniques for exploring it, connecting it to other knowledge bases, and making practical use of it. In other words, the landscape upon which we used to stand has been transformed, and we are being forced to establish a new foundation called information literacy. Now knowledge—not minerals or agricultural products or manufactured goods—is this country's most precious commodity, and people who are information literate—who know how to acquire knowledge and use it—are America's most valuable resource" (American Library Association Presidential Committee on Information Literacy, 1989, p. 10).

Information literacy is emerging as one of the most critical literacies for an educated person who will be living and working in the twenty-first century. While the graduation of students who are information literate and experienced in resource-based learning should, therefore, be one of the most obvious and easily agreed on goals for higher education, the majority of American colleges have not yet actively responded.

Faculty, librarians, and students have yet to embrace the attitudinal and behavioral changes necessary for making information literacy and resource-based learning a priority and a reality in higher education. The attitudinal change is a vital prerequisite for the graduation of students who are information literate and practitioners of resource-based learning. It calls for nothing less than a rethinking of educational priorities and strategies. It requires redefinition of values and transformation of an existing campus culture to act on a new set of principles.

To bring about this change, faculty, librarians, and students must first redefine their roles. Faculty members must see themselves less as disseminators of information in the classroom and more as facilitators who empower students to become autonomous learners through involvement in resource-based learning outside of the classroom. Librarians need to become less the guardians of information and more the coaches who develop within students the capacity not only to access information but also to evaluate and choose information. Students need to turn away from being passive and dependent learners and become active and independent learners who are able to bring to the classroom information that they have critically selected and analyzed. Most important, all three groups should recognize that information literacy requires establishment of an active partnership in a genuine learning community.

Barriers for Faculty

Most faculty define themselves professionally within the context of the subject matter and methodology of their respective disciplines. They value their special knowledge highly and perceive authority and respect as tied to possession and control of that knowledge. Implementation of an information literacy program requires faculty to discover new ways to disseminate and share that knowledge with students. At the present time, faculty also depend largely on the textbook and the lecture, which are expertly processed and prepackaged bits of information for easy student digestion. The challenges of the Information Age and of resource-based learning, however, demand that faculty develop teaching strategies that help students become evaluators, critical readers, and users of information that they individually, and in collaboration with faculty, discover. Faculty need to help students become autonomous learners who understand the value of integrating the increasing number of information resources available throughout society and the world as linked by new communications technology.

Some frequently heard comments of faculty provide insights into many of the specific barriers that they need to overcome in order to implement information literacy and resource-based learning programs. Most of these barriers are attitudinal blocks that prevent faculty from changing their behavior.

Insufficient Time. Faculty who teach subject matter courses frequently feel that they do not have sufficient class time to help students develop information literacy skills. These faculty are caught in two traps: the belief that there is a finite body of information that must be transferred in an information-rich environment through the traditional lecture method and the belief that information literacy is something added on rather than thoroughly integrated into the curriculum. These faculty members run the risk of becoming academic dinosaurs in the midst of an information age that threatens to pass them by. Just as nineteenth-century artists responded to the challenge presented by the invention of the camera, faculty today need to redefine their roles due to advances in information technology. For their own as well as for their students' benefit, faculty need to differentiate their role from that of the textbook—developing understanding and valuing process skills rather than disseminating prepackaged information and rewarding memorization skills.

Information literacy cannot be effectively implemented as an add-on to a course or to a curriculum. It needs to be thoroughly integrated into the design of courses and reflected in objectives for both individual courses and the entire curriculum. Faculty members should pose questions that require students to engage in resource-based learning in order to help them develop within the dynamic environment of the classroom the capacity to select and to evaluate information appropriate for formulating answers. These expectations need to govern the design of assignments and the use of class time. An effective information literacy program should not compete with the use of class time but instead complement it and help students to respond successfully to more challenging assignments.

Tried It and It Does Not Work. There are three basic reasons for why information literacy programs do not work: failure to provide students with appropriate instruction, failure to understand the necessary collaborative effort between faculty and librarians, and failure to see the program and its courses as part of an entire curriculum—part of a plan of learning. Faculty should not expect students to acquire information literacy on their own. Students should be systematically introduced to the variety of resources in a discipline through the design of pretested assignments. Faculty members need to know in advance that the principal resources for an assignment are available in the library or easily accessible through interlibrary loan or electronic data bases. Pretesting of assignments enables faculty to understand in advance some of the possible difficulties that students will encounter in finding the correct descriptors for locating information through computerized data bases and printed sources. Faculty members need to be certain that they are information literate before establishing this expectation for their students.

Faculty members should also understand that implementation of a meaningful information literacy program requires a partnership with librarians. Faculty need to accept librarians as colleagues, as educators, and as professional equals. Faculty members who share their course objectives with librarians are likely to find that librarians can offer suggestions on a variety of assignments and classroom activities to engage students in active learning.

Faculty should also recognize that students cannot acquire information literacy by an individual faculty member's efforts in a single class. Information literacy is a developmental process that students need to experience over all four years of undergraduate education and throughout an entire curriculum. This need requires faculty to initiate a truly collegial approach across courses and even departments so that students experience resource-based learning and information literacy sequentially, developmentally, and comprehensively. The most effective learning takes place for students when faculty consciously build on prior learning. When faculty think and act in concert, they have the power to transform a collection of courses into a plan of learning.

"Not My Problem." These are the saddest words of all. They reveal a faculty that is teacher-centered rather than student-centered, a faculty whose allegiance is so exclusively tied to their disciplines that they have abandoned their role as educators. Faculty members need to include assignments that involve resource-based learning if they are serious about helping students learn how to learn. This assistance cannot be offered by encouraging students to rely on predigested textbook information and lecture notes. The challenge for today's students is not the scarcity of information but the abundance of information. New and more sophisticated skills of analysis are required if students are to achieve information literacy. In an information-rich environment it is only through resource-based learning that students can become self-directed learners who are prepared to successfully pursue the goal of lifelong learning. If development of information literacy for students is not a priority goal for faculty, then faculty are not being honest when they urge that the library be made central to student learning. And without information literacy goals, the library is relegated to being a study hall. Faculty need to pay more attention to the specific learning goals and actual learning outcomes for assignments in relationship to course and curriculum goals. Low faculty expectations in information literacy for student learning are a barrier to student achievement of the kind of autonomy as learners that should be the objective of every faculty member.

Another factor contributing to this barrier is the degree to which faculty define the challenge of developing information literacy for students as a problem belonging exclusively to librarians. Faculty should have learned years ago from the writing-across-the-curriculum movement that mastery requires students to develop a skill in all disciplines over all four years of education. Moreover, students will never become effective writers if the task is left only to English faculty in freshman composition courses.

Faculty need to transfer this insight to the challenge of helping students acquire information literacy skills.

As far as other barriers for faculty are concerned, institutions need to respond to the faculty's perception of the reward structure. Who and what will reward faculty who involve students in resource-based learning and information literacy activities?

Barriers for Librarians

The barriers for librarians regarding resource-based learning and information literacy are less immediately apparent but no less real. The lower visibility of the barriers for librarians is perhaps due to a shared recognition that they are the information specialists and have a vested interest in serving the information needs of students.

Just as faculty must rethink the use of class time and the design of assignments, librarians need to rethink the learning environment within libraries and the prerequisites for establishing an effective partnership with faculty. The traditional learning environment associated with libraries has conditioned students to perceive the library as a quiet study hall or the sacred space of a place of worship. Neither image is appropriate for students who are actively pursuing information through reference services and electronic data bases and learning from peers. Faculty increasingly expect students to engage in cooperative research projects in which learning through interaction with peers is incorporated into the design of assignments. The pursuit of resource-based learning and information literacy must be conducted in an interactive environment. Strong interpersonal skills of librarians play a key role in promoting an interactive environment and implementing an effective information literacy program. Although librarians want increasingly to encourage this active level of communication, libraries all too frequently have a traditional physical design that inhibits users. The reference area is becoming a hub of activity filled with the voices of humans and machines, which creates discomfort for students who feel that they are invading the quiet space of others. Librarians need to create a new environment by reconfiguring existing space and technology as well as by making the library as user-friendly as possible.

Librarians also have an obligation to attend to the prerequisites for establishing an effective partnership with faculty. An effective partnership should be based on faculty recognition of librarians as educators. Unfortunately, this recognition is rare among faculty since they view with suspicion educators who are not in the classroom. A starting point for correcting the misperceptions of faculty is for librarians to devise and participate in collaborative activities that underscore their unique role as information educators. Many faculty are not aware of the dramatic changes that have recently taken place in the area of information science in regard to the availability of resources and new search strategies to both faculty and students. Simultaneously, librarians need to communicate their special expertise to enhance faculty efforts in implementing resource-based learning for students.

Some of the specific barriers for librarians seeking to contribute to resource-based learning and information literacy on college campuses deserve greater exposure on campus. These are important barriers that faculty and students need to know exist and librarians need to resolve.

Demands Are Already Too Great. Most college libraries are understaffed to meet current demands of patrons. How is it possible for librarians to meet the increased demands for services generated by resource-based learning and information literacy programs? The answer is that it is not possible if librarians view themselves as exclusively responsible for responding to these increased demands. One of the advantages of a partnership with faculty is that an appropriate portion of this responsibility can be assumed by faculty. Assignments need to be jointly designed by faculty and librarians to determine in advance their feasibility relative to resources available in the library. A collaborative effort also guarantees that librarians understand the objectives of faculty course assignments. Librarians should never be surprised by student inquiries. Faculty members also can be available in the library at key moments to assist their students. In large universities, graduate students can also be utilized to assist undergraduates in learning how to use computerized data bases and initiative search strategies.

Librarians might also reduce demands on their expertise in relation to repetitive reference questions by producing pamphlets and reference or study guides on such topics as how to use government documents and how to write an annotated bibliography. These pamphlets can be featured in the reference area of the library. Libraries that make these introductory guides available frequently find that these materials serve both to reduce the quantity of repetitive questions and to increase the quality of subsequent reference questions. The guides also increase the sense of partnership between librarians and faculty, especially if faculty refer students to the appropriate guides when making assignments. The consequence of these strategies can be that reference librarians become resources for answering high-quality reference questions, those that students should come to ask in a truly successful information literacy program.

In the Information Age, it is also appropriate to question whether all librarians should become primarily reference librarians. To what extent can other necessary but repetitive library functions be carried out by trained paraprofessionals under the supervision of a librarian? This is not only a question of efficiency but, more important, one of effectiveness. Increasingly, libraries in the twenty-first century will have to become information centers.

Students Not Interested. Most observers and participants in traditional bibliographic instruction programs would be quick to express their disappointment in the current learning outcomes for students. This disappointment does not mean that these programs cannot be made effective. It does mean, however, that they need to be thoroughly reformulated, with a student's perspective in mind since interest precedes learning for most students.

The apparent lack of interest of students in traditional library instruction programs does not reflect lack of interest in learning but rather lack of relevance in the goals and designs of traditional programs. The most effective way to change this attitude is to abandon the idea that information literacy programs can accomplish their goals by providing generic instruction. Library instruction needs to be discipline-specific. It also needs to be course-specific and curriculum-specific at the time when students have a need for the information and instruction. Librarians and faculty can design programs that target key courses over all four years of education and thus provide students with a systematic and developmentally designed approach to resources and search strategies in their major fields of study. Clearly, a collaborative spirit among faculty and librarians is essential to realizing this goal.

Many traditional programs have evolved out of library orientation programs designed to help students physically move through the library collection and services, a goal that focuses on the library as a place. The higher-order reasoning goals embedded in resource-based learning and information literacy demand that the library be viewed as a concept and as a process.

Barriers for Students

Barriers that prevent students from realizing the goals of resource-based learning and information literacy arise primarily from student conditioning to be passive rather than active learners. Students do not enter college as independent learners. Therefore, it is not surprising that faculty expectations for students in regard to resource-based learning and information literacy are both foreign and frightening.

It may also serve as an indicator of the qualitative decline in American education that students have grown comfortable in their role as passive learners. They easily define their role as consumers of prepackaged and predigested information through lectures and through textbooks. They fear active learning both because they lack prior experience and because they lack the required degree of self-confidence. Effective programs in information literacy must recognize where first-year students are as learners upon entering college and establish a specific plan to help students evolve toward meeting the expectations appropriate for graduating seniors. Students need to understand that faculty and librarians can be facilitators of learning, but that students are the only ones who can make learning happen.

Some of the specific barriers for students to overcome in order to successfully engage in resource-based learning and information literacy programs reflect students' peculiar sense that education is a product to be consumed rather than a process into which they enter. Resource-based learning and information literacy are excellent strategies for correcting this misunderstanding.

Not Important. Most students are not sophisticated enough or knowledgeable enough about the implications of the transition to the Information Age to understand the importance of resource-based learning and information literacy. Their knowledge of the world of work is frequently limited to traditional careers pursued by family members and friends. They are not looking to the future. They are not likely to see that the future world of work will demand they have the capacity to make connections among a variety of information resources. The majority of American workers in the twenty-first century will pursue careers directly related to the identification, selection, analysis, application, and communication of information. Even now, business leaders call for college graduates who are critical thinkers and problem solvers and who are able to search out and process information from throughout the global community.

Too Difficult. Students who have grown comfortable with passive modes of instruction are reluctant to disturb this level of comfort by accepting the challenge of becoming active learners. But it is not only the comfort level that is involved here. It is also an unwillingness to take a risk. It is not that faculty expectations are beyond the ability of students to successfully respond. It is more the case that students are attracted to what is easiest. Even when students use the new tools of information technology, there are disturbing signs of their unwillingness to exert themselves. Faculty complain frequently that when using computerized data bases in searches, students limit their searches to the years included in the data bases and do not continue to search manually in the printed indexes for material from earlier years.

Students' tendency to gravitate toward what is the easiest can be changed only by faculty who create higher expectations and hold students accountable, not only in individual courses but also throughout the entire curriculum. An individual family member cannot accomplish this change alone. It requires a cooperative approach involving the majority of faculty. Only when confronted by faculty solidarity will students accept their responsibility to engage in resource-based learning and to achieve information literacy.

Teacher's Responsibility. Years of experiencing passive modes of instruction have convinced many students that learning is the responsibility of the teacher, not of the student. No wonder students resist becoming involved in resource-based learning and information literacy, since both require that they take the primary responsibility for their own learning. The very idea that students need to identify, select, evaluate, and organize information for use in the classroom is unsettling and threatening to many students.

Reliance on passive modes of instruction has encouraged students to become dependent rather than independent learners. This claim strikes a discordant note with educational reformers who argue that the quality of education increasingly needs to be judged in terms of the extent to which the resources for learning have been adequate to develop students who are self-confident, independent learners.

Challenge of Technology

Technology poses both a promise for and a threat to information literacy. The promise lies in its ability to radically shrink global society by making information from all cultures available to everyone. It also makes the information resources of large university libraries readily available to students at small colleges.

The threat posed by technology on most college campuses is its cost. Technology is commanding an increasingly larger share of the budget, and the realization that existing technology must continuously be replaced in the future is frightening. Administrators must understand, nevertheless, that the long-run cost of not moving ahead with technology in the service of information literacy is even greater—further decline in the quality of higher education and in America's competitiveness in the world.

Colleges and universities can take a number of steps to reduce current and future costs. First, administrators must admit that libraries cannot and should not be expected to have all of the available resources. Interlibrary loan services and electronic data bases need to become the most visible and active library services on every campus. Resource networks need to be established to encourage a cooperative use of existing information resources. This idea, however, is only practical if sufficient funds are available to compensate the lending institutions. Librarians also need to understand that the level of technology should clearly distinguish between an undergraduate library and a library serving graduate programs. Librarians at undergraduate institutions need to exercise the necessary self-restraint to skip several stages of technology upgrades until such time as the required expenditures result in a significant improvement for users. Finally, every college needs to develop a comprehensive technology plan that not only sets directions but also provides for annual contributions to an equipment replacement fund from an operating budget that spreads the cost of technology purchases over more than a single fiscal year.

Conclusion

What will it mean to be educated in the twenty-first century? The answer is complex and generates diverse responses. But information literacy and resource-based learning are common elements among the responses of those seriously confronting the challenges of the Information Age.

The American Library Association Presidential Committee on Information Literacy (1989, p. 1) defined an information literate person as one who recognizes when information is needed and is able to locate, evaluate, and use effectively the needed information: "Ultimately, information literate people are those who have learned how to learn. They know how to learn because they know how information is organized, how to find information, and how to use information in such a way that others can learn from them. They are people prepared for lifelong learning, because they can always find the information needed for any task or decision at hand." Faculty, librarians, and students can successfully meet this challenge by recognizing the new roles that each is required to play. The first step in overcoming barriers is to recognize that they exist. The next step is to begin the process of attitudinal change that informs behavioral change. Successful change to achieve information literacy and resource-based learning requires a collaborative effort among faculty, librarians, and students and the establishment of a learning community for an information-rich environment. Quality education requires going beyond the rhetoric of excellence to the implementation of programs that transform rhetoric into reality.

Reference

American Library Association Presidential Committee on Information Literacy. *Final Report.* Chicago: American Library Association, 1989.

D. W. FARMER is vice president for academic affairs at King's College, Wilkes-Barre, Pennsylvania.

An increasing number of faculty are calling for a substantive transformation of education with resource-based learning at its new core.

Transforming Campus Culture Through Resource-Based Learning

James L. Pence

Anthropologist Clifford Geertz (1983, p. 20) writes, "Something is happening to the way we think about the way we think." Geertz hypothesizes that social thought is being "reconfigured" and that the traditional lines of distinction dividing scholarly disciplines are being "blurred" by the creation of new kinds of intellectual communities where the focus is on "contextual relations." Geertz posits a "change in our notion not so much of what knowledge is but of what it is we want to know" (p. 34).

Stanley Aronowitz and Henry Giroux (1991, p. 187), a sociologist and an education professor, respectively, write that the decade of the 1980s was marked by "the emergence of two crosscurrents that appear paradoxical from the standpoint of traditional social and cultural theory." One current is the conservative "back-to-the-basics" approach based on a curriculum of canonical texts and an educational system focused on questions of accountability. The other is the "postmodern" current, which "links schooling to democratic public life, that defines teachers as engaged intellectuals and border crossers, and develops forms of pedagogy that incorporate difference, plurality, and the language of the everyday as central to the production and legitimation of learning" (p. 187).

Psychologist K. Patricia Cross (1990, p. 16) believes that "education, properly understood, is not so much additive as transformational." A developer and advocate of classroom research, Cross calls for fulfillment in the 1990s of the reforms anticipated in the 1980s: direct involvement of faculty in continuing development as teachers; joining knowledge of subject matter with knowledge of teaching within disciplinary contexts; and reducing the gap between research and practice.

Philosopher Elizabeth Minnich (1990, p. 31), analyzing the "conceptual errors that lock the dominant meaning system shaping liberal arts curricula into exclusive, invidiously hierarchical sets of structures, values, principles, beliefs, and feelings," argues for a "transformed knowledge" to "help us all envision and actually experience moments in which the possibility of the intimate, universal communication that is the transforming heart of publicly responsible learning comes alive" (p. 187).

Bellah and others (1985, pp. 286, 289) call for a "transition to a new level of social integration" to make us "aware of our intricate connectedness and interdependence." Bellah and others (1991, p. 279) analyzed American institutions, including education, and call for a new "moral paradigm—a paradigm of cultivation" to replace the reliance on individualism as the basis for American democracy. "One becomes what one knows," they assert (1991, p. 158). And what one knows is determined, in large part, by the company one keeps. Accordingly, colleges should become learning communities where the cooperative and interactive nature of learning replaces the "individualistic competition of students pitted against each other for high places on the grade curve" (p. 172).

The Call for Transformation

What do all of these writers and thinkers have in common? Their voices are among an increasing number of teachers and professors calling for a substantive transformation of our entire system of education with resource-based learning at its new core. For them, reformation is not enough. Not every one of the voices refers specifically to the concept of resource-based learning in calling for change, but the general principles underlying their messages are eminently compatible. As we use knowledge, the challenge is to connect rather than to dissect, the object is to interpret rather than to explain, and the task is to interrogate and render critical judgment rather than to analyze. With resource-based learning, student experience is central, the teacher is viewed as an intellectual, and the purpose of education is to create meaning, not to train for a career.

The wrong question to ask is, What can institutions do to support resource-based learning? A better question is, How will the integration of resource-based learning into the contexts of an institution bring about the kind of cultural change that transforms?

The Leadership Challenge

In an age of competition for limited resources, any call to transform campus culture through resource-based learning, no matter how impassioned, will likely go unheeded. Too many needs claim our attention, and cultural change is more difficult to accomplish than are changes in systems or procedures. In spite of our rhetoric and our intentions, many of us in higher education prefer tactical planning to strategic. We are typically more concerned with short-term fixes and quick results than with long-term solutions. Like American society in general, we are more comfortable with exploitation than cultivation; therefore, institutional change does not come easily (Bellah and others, 1991, p. 272). For transformation of campus culture to occur, academic leaders (faculty and administrators) must accept the leadership challenge to cultivate a climate for cultural change and demonstrate resource-based learning.

From my perspective as an academic dean of a liberal arts college, the leadership challenge to transform campus culture through resource-based learning involves the creation and nurturance of a campus environment wherein faculty *and* academic administrators form collaborative learning communities and become "mutually intelligible interpreters" (Bellah and others, 1991, p. 172). The ecology of this environment is most fittingly described by the existence of three necessary cultural conditions; coincidentally and significantly, these are the same three conditions that the National Institute of Education (1984) recommended to improve the quality of students' undergraduate education: involvement, high expectations, and assessment and feedback.

Involvement. The National Institute of Education (1984) offers seven recommendations for increasing student involvement as a collective prerequisite to improving undergraduate education. Recommendation 5 states, "Every institution of higher education should strive to create learning communities, organized around specific intellectual themes or tasks"; a proposed feature of these learning communities is that faculty "relate to one another both as specialists and as educators" (1984, p. 33).

While the National Institute of Education envisions learning communities composed of faculty and students functioning as co-inquirers, I imagine the formation of complementary communities consisting of faculty and academic administrators who see themselves primarily as educators. Faculty often have difficulty relating to one another and to administrators as educators. In academe today, "teaching is widely undervalued" (Seldin and Associates, 1990, p. 199). The academic department, long the bastion of parochial territorialism, contributes to the undervaluation of teaching by encouraging deification of the disciplines. "It is the reification and reductionism of education into the study of disciplines that make them into inert objects of adoration" (Purpel, 1989, p. 153). For Aronowitz and Giroux (1991, pp. 140, 142), "The historical basis of the disciplines has been largely overturned," and "the object of knowledge subordinated to explorations of ways of knowing." The Association of American Colleges (1990, p. 20) believes that "one of the chief causes for the disarray of the curriculum and the demise of good teaching was the increased professionalism of the professoriate and faculty development of primary loyalties to their disciplines rather than to the institutions where they taught or to their students."

And yet, in many colleges and universities, faculty relate to one another primarily within academic departments and typically not as *educators*. Faculty organize themselves into groups for bureaucratic, collegial, political, or symbolic purposes; "pedagogical" is significantly absent from the list (Birnbaum, 1991).

Meaningful faculty involvement in the cultivation of a campus environment that places resource-based learning at its core will come about when faculty and administrators become "critical co-investigators in dialogue" (Freire, 1989, p. 68). Just as Freire's teacher-students and student-teachers "become jointly responsible for a process in which all grow" (p. 69), faculty-administrator communities must learn to engage in dialogue about issues that matter for students and for themselves. They must "struggle collectively as transformative intellectuals, that is, as educators who have a social vision and commitment . . . , the courage to take risks, to look into the future, and to imagine a world that could be as opposed to simply what is" (Giroux, 1988, p. 215).

A good example of the envisioned faculty-administrator relations is described by Cochran (1989), who believes that institutional effectiveness depends on a joint commitment from faculty and administrators to the task of improving teaching. If a faculty-administrative group were to read Cochran's book together, enter into dialogue about it, and assume the role of problem-posing educators whose goal is to strengthen teaching on their own campus, the cultural condition of involvement would be nurtured and, by extension, a campus environment hospitable to resource-based learning created. Boyer's (1987, 1990) works could also be studied profitably by faculty and administrators. Although Boyer's books have circulated widely through higher education, and many faculty and administrators have read them, I do not believe that they have been used often as the basis for faculty-administrative dialogue about issues that matter. A third example is an institution's engagement in the act of revising faculty personnel policies as "a collaborative writing project performed by institutional ethnographers who are creating or recreating the 'story' the institution tells itself about itself" (Pence, 1990, p. 60).

Unfortunately, Bellah and others (1991, pp. 176-177) provide an exceptionally accurate assessment of higher education. Higher education has expanded in ways that individuals cannot any longer understand. To overcome disciplinary specialization, so many interdisciplinary programs, projects, and institutes have been created that they only increase the level of incoherence. Most university faculty are more oriented to their disciplines than to the institutions' educational purposes. It will take extraordinary leadership to get faculty to think about the educational implications of what they are doing. A greater awareness of the larger educational issues among the faculty of our most prestigious institutions is probably a precondition for successful institutional innovation. That greater awareness is needed at all institutions. It is more likely to come about through resource-based approaches by faculty-administrative learning communities than through other more traditional routes.

The involvement condition assumes that we cannot ask students to do something we are unwilling or unable to do ourselves. If we expect students to become resource-based learners, we must model the behavior that we wish to nurture. This modeling will not happen through the traditional organizational structure of the academic department. It may, however, occur if faculty and administrators form learning communities without regard to disciplinary boundaries and involve themselves in the intellectual act of making meaning through dialogue about students and about teaching, scholarship, and service. "Dialogue—loving, humble, and full of faith"— produces a "climate of mutual trust, which leads the dialoguers into ever closer partnerships" (Freire, 1989, p. 80). Support of resource-based learning on campus means that faculty and administrators become resource-based learners.

High Expectations. Many times have I heard in a meeting, "If it ain't broke, don't fix it." Now, I usually give the response, "If it ain't broke, you just haven't looked hard enough. Fix it anyway" (Peters, 1987, p. 3). The National Institute of Education (1984) lists eight recommendations for realizing high expectations, for faculty as teachers and scholars and for students as learners. Each of these recommendations, if adopted, would lead to the cultivation of a climate hospitable to resource-based learning for students. Recommendation 8 states, "Faculties and chief academic officers in each institution should agree upon and disseminate a statement of the knowledge, capacities, and skills that students must develop prior to graduation" (1984, p. 39).

With few exceptions, statements of high expectations have not been as meaningfully adapted to faculty and administrators as they have to students in the aftermath of *Involvement in Learning: Realizing the Potential of American Higher Education* (National Institute of Education, 1984). Encouraging developments in recent years, however, point to faculty-administrator adaptation. For example, Santa Fe Community College created a faculty-based project to establish effective teaching criteria in support of goals related to student success. In developing their criteria, Santa Fe faculty agreed that instructor effectiveness should be measured in terms of expectations for faculty competence in critical thinking, subject knowledge, communication skills, inducement of a climate favorable for learning, classroom management, and self-conscious reflection on a variety of teaching methods (Weimer, 1991).

Seldin (1991, p. 3) adapts the portfolio concept to higher education and shows how faculty can "display their teaching accomplishments for examination by others" and thereby "raise individual and collective performance levels in the classroom." Faculty in the College of Business Administration at Georgia State University have developed a multiple-paths evaluation system that allows faculty members to develop individual profiles that establish their own high expectations; department chairs then evaluate faculty members against their own profiles, not in competition with other faculty (Brightman and others, 1990). In Svinicki (1990), ten chapters focus exclusively on the changing face of college teaching. A survey of some of the chapter titles illustrates the scope of the changes described: "Collaborative Learning: Shared Inquiry as a Process of Reform," "Teaching with Cases: Learning to Question," "Assessing and Improving Students' Learning Strategies," and " 'Study' Your Way to Better Teaching." In these chapters, the argument centers on the establishment of reasonable, measurable, and meaningful expectations for individual and collective faculty performance.

To cultivate an environment hospitable to resource-based learning, faculty and chief academic officers should agree on and disseminate a statement of the specific expectations for faculty performance as teachers-scholars. These expectations should include faculty goals for their own learning, as based on the faculty member's acquisition of a level of information literacy appropriate for the individual's teaching responsibility and as demonstrated through teaching, scholarship, and service.

Furthermore, faculty and chief academic officers should collaborate on the design of faculty development programs that reinforce the resource-based learning approach (both for faculty to use themselves and to apply in the classroom). Perhaps it is time for institutions to give at least as much support to teams of faculty who wish to attend conferences on improving teaching as they do to individual professors who present scholarly papers at disciplinary meetings. Faculty-based initiatives to expand the library's collection on pedagogy are long overdue. Development programs to teach faculty to use electronic data bases, hypermedia, and computing to improve teaching should be welcomed on campuses and given priority in resource allocations.

Finally, faculty and chief academic officers should collaborate on the design and implementation of administrator development programs. Academic officers are typically expected by their faculty to keep current on the issues affecting higher education; those who do meet such expectations are more likely to endorse resource-based learning than those who do not. Academic deans carry a special responsibility to model the behavior that they are trying to encourage by functioning as active resource-based learners. Administrator development programs help to create a campus culture that recognizes the need for "mutually intelligible interpreters." Support of research-based learning on campus means investment in the human potential of faculty and administrators, who also must function and interact as lifelong learners.

Assessment and Feedback. The National Institute of Education (1984, p. 21) offers five recommendations on the "use of assessment information to redirect effort" and serve "as a powerful lever for involvement." Institutions' values are often revealed by the information that they gather and use. Regional accreditation bodies, professional associations, learned societies, and state governments have jumped on the assessment bandwagon in an effort to improve the quality of undergraduate education by designing systems to measure institutional effectiveness and student outcomes. Less attention is paid to information about faculty and administrator growth and development between entry into the profession and separation from it.

Faculty and administrators who have read Katz and Henry (1988) or Nelsen (1981) know something about the importance of faculty development to the success of the educational enterprise. But until the relatively recent emphasis on the use of teaching portfolios (Seldin and Associates, 1990; Seldin, 1991), little attention had been paid to documentation of faculty growth; virtually no literature exists on the topic of developing administrators as learners. Because portfolios are both process and outcome, they focus an individual's attention on self-perceptions of growth and require that personal assertions about abilities be supported by evidence collected over time. Because they include personal narrative, portfolios encourage one to become "self-critical about the historically constructed nature of one's experience" (Giroux, 1988, p. 153).

To cultivate a climate that integrates resource-based learning into the fabric of the institution, faculty and administrators should agree on the kinds of information to be collected about each other's activities and abilities over time. They should agree on how that information will be used to redirect their efforts and serve as a lever for involvement and an incentive for improvement.

In the 1980s, institutional planning came to mean strategic planning: "the process of developing and maintaining a strategic fit between the organization and its changing market opportunities" (Kotler and Murphy, 1981, p. 471). In a strategic planning model, choice of a strategic direction results from key decisions about institutional mission, clientele, programs and services, comparative advantages, and institutional goals and objectives. Strategic analysis begins with institutional assessments of the threats and opportunities in the external environment, strengths and weaknesses in the internal environment, and values held within the organization (Shirley, 1983). Rarely has assessment of individual growth and professional development been linked to institutional planning.

In the 1990s, we should apply the principles of strategic planning to human resources development through a process of establishing and maintaining a strategic fit between the organization and its employees. This process might involve each member of a learning community preparing an inventory of his or her own activities *and* abilities as part of the portfolio and together sharing those inventories with one another. The community then seeks to match individual abilities with group or organizational needs so that self-generated information becomes the guiding principle for developing and maintaining strategic fit between the individual and the organization. A set of inventories for teaching effectiveness might look like the following:

Activities Inventory

Directions: Write a brief description of your activities as a teacher over the past year, referring (for example) to

- The courses you taught
- The number and types of students you taught
- The changes you made in your courses from previous times that you taught them
- Any experimental or special strategies that you used
- Any use of nonprint media
- Any use of resources beyond the textbook and syllabus materials that you prepared

Abilities Inventory

Directions: Using information provided by your own self-assessment, student perceptions, and/or colleague evaluations, describe your abilities in each outcomes category.

1. Intellectual skills (writing, speaking, listening, reading, problem solving, information gathering)
2. Intellectual capacities (analysis, synthesis, inferential reasoning, critical thinking)
3. Knowledge (discipline based, general education, interdisciplinary studies)

If faculty in the learning community share an annual Activities-Abilities Inventory with each other and if those inventories are assessed by the community within the contexts of institutional plans, group members would be providing one another with valuable feedback. Working in collaboration, the members of the group develop and maintain a strategic match between group members and the organization, nurturing an environment conducive to resource-based learning. Ultimately, support of resource-based learning on campus becomes a matter of providing structured opportunities for information sharing among individuals who collaborate with one another in the matching of individual abilities to group and organizational needs.

Summary

To support research-based learning on campus, institutional leaders from the faculty and the administration must function as learning communities that collaborate to model and practice the behavior that they expect from their students. They must encourage one another and their students to become border crossers. Increasing specialization within already specialized disciplines and the "knowledge explosion" make the challenge of integrating learning difficult, a challenge that the authors of almost every reform report issued in the 1980s agree we must meet. Significantly, one of the earliest reform reports of the 1990s calls for "faculty commitment to curricular coherence, critical perspectives, and connected learning . . . [to provide] an overarching framework through which programs can examine their practices and research for full participation of all students in arts and sciences fields" (Association of American Colleges, 1991, p. 17).

Information literacy and use of technology for access to information will not be sufficient to bring about the creation of a resource-based learning environment. Nothing short of the transformation of campus cultures to cultivate habits of the mind known as critical literacy will bring positive results. Resource-based learning, with its emphasis on the learning process, the experiences of the everyday world, and the empowerment of learners as engaged intellectuals, has the power to transform campus culture and to help us decide, together, what it is that we really want to know. Through resource-based approaches, the paradigm of cultivation can replace the paradigm of exploitation (Bellah and others, 1991), and colleges can exist as sites of transformed knowledge inhabited by mutually intelligible interpreters for whom knowing leads meaningfully to becoming.

References

Aronowitz, S., and Giroux, H. *Postmodern Education: Politics, Culture, and Social Criticism.* Minneapolis: University of Minnesota Press, 1991.

Association of American Colleges. *Integrity in the College Curriculum: A Report to the Academic Community.* Washington, D.C.: Association of American Colleges, 1990.

Association of American Colleges. *The Challenge of Connected Learning.* Washington, D.C.: Association of American Colleges, 1991.

Bellah, R., and others. *Habits of the Heart.* New York: HarperCollins, 1985.

Bellah, R., and others. *The Good Society.* New York: Knopf, 1991.

Birnbaum, R. "The Latent Organizational Functions of the Academic Senate: Why Senates Do Not Work but Will Not Go Away." In R. Birnbaum (ed.), *Faculty in Governance: The Role of Senates and Joint Committees in Academic Decision Making.* New Directions for Higher Education, no. 75. San Francisco: Jossey-Bass, 1991.

Boyer, E. L. *College: The Undergraduate Experience in America.* New York: HarperCollins, 1987.

Boyer, E. L. *Scholarship Preconsidered: Priorities of the Professoriate.* Princeton, N.J.: Carnegie Foundation for the Advancement of Teaching, 1990.

Brightman, H., and others. "The Multiple-Paths Faculty Evaluation System." *Journal on Excellence in College Teaching,* 1990, *1,* 109-117.

Cochran, L. *Administrative Commitment to Teaching: Practical Research-Based Strategies to Strengthen College Teaching Effectiveness.* Cape Girardeau, Mo.: STEP UP, 1989.

Cross, K. P. "Teaching to Improve Learning." *Journal on Excellence in College Teaching,* 1990, *1,* 9-22.

Freire, P. *Pedagogy of the Oppressed.* New York: Continuum, 1989.

Geertz, C. "Blurred Genres: The Reconfiguration of Social Thought." In C. Geertz, *Local Knowledge: Further Essays in Interpretive Anthropology.* New York: Basic Books, 1983.

Giroux, H. *Schooling and the Struggle for Public Life.* Minneapolis: University of Minnesota Press, 1988.

Katz, J., and Henry, M. *Turning Professors into Teachers: A New Approach to Faculty Development and Student Learning.* New York: American Council on Education and Macmillan, 1988.

Kotler, P., and Murphy, P. "Strategic Planning for Higher Education." *Journal of Higher Education,* 1981, *52* (5), 470-489.

Minnich, E. K. *Transforming Knowledge.* Philadelphia: Temple University Press, 1990.

National Institute of Education. Study Group on the Conditions of Excellence in American Higher Education. *Involvement in Learning: Realizing the Potential of American Higher Education.* Washington, D.C.: Government Printing Office, 1984.

Nelsen, W. C. *Renewal of the Teacher-Scholar: Faculty Development in the Liberal Arts College.* Washington, D.C.: Association of American Colleges, 1981.

Pence, J. L. "Adapting Faculty Personnel Policies." In D. W. Steeples (ed.), *Managing Change in Higher Education.* New Directions for Higher Education, no. 71. San Francisco: Jossey-Bass, 1990.

Peters, T. *Thriving on Chaos.* New York: HarperCollins, 1987.

Purpel, D. *The Moral and Spiritual Crisis in Education.* Granby, Mass.: Begin & Garvey, 1989.

Seldin, P. *The Teaching Portfolio: A Practical Guide to Improved Performance and Promotion/Tenure Decisions.* Bolton, Maine: Anker, 1991.

Seldin, P., and Associates. *How Administrators Can Improve Teaching: Moving from Talk to Action in Higher Education.* San Francisco: Jossey-Bass, 1990.

Shirley, R. "Identifying the Levels of Strategy for a College or University." *Long Range Planning,* 1983, *16* (3), 92-96.

Svinicki, M. D. (ed.). *The Changing Face of College Teaching.* New Directions for Teaching and Learning, no. 42. San Francisco: Jossey-Bass, 1990.

Weimer, M. "Effective Instruction: The Quest to Define It at Santa Fe Community College." *Teaching Professor,* 1991, *5* (10), 3-4.

JAMES L. PENCE is vice president for academic affairs and dean of the faculty at Wartburg College, Waverly, Iowa.

Afterword

D. W. Farmer (1990) observed in an earlier volume of New Directions for Higher Education that change always carries with it a sense of violation and this invites resistance. Yet, change and adaptation are two essential requirements for institutional survival and academic growth. The definition of literacy has changed to incorporate information literacy developed through resource-based learning. This kind of literacy will be one of the necessary survival skills for those who will be living and working in the twenty-first century. The challenge for higher education today is to employ to good purpose the conservative instinct to preserve what is most valuable in its pedagogical tradition and at the same time introduce the changes required in an information-rich environment. Colleges and universities have an obligation to help students become independent learners. This goal can be achieved by enabling students to bring critical thinking and problem-solving skills to the acquisition, integration, and evaluation of information.

The development of students as independent learners ought to be central to the mission of institutions of higher education. But it is necessary to go beyond the rhetoric frequently associated with this goal by systematically changing the way faculty, librarians, and students think about and act on their respective roles in education. Information literacy has the potential to redefine the educated person in the twenty-first century and to increase both the quality and the quantity of student learning. The strategy of resource-based learning, complemented by the traditional liberal learning skills of critical thinking and effective communication, requires students to become active learners who can achieve academic self-confidence and independence. Faculty and librarians need to empower students by implementing resource-based learning and by developing their coaching skills. The well-known adage that more is gained by teaching a man to fish than by giving him a fish is apropos when thinking about the purpose of and implementation strategies for an information literacy program.

Common Themes

The contributors to this volume have shared a variety of unique campus-based experiences relating to information literacy and resource-based learning. But lying beneath the uniqueness of each experience are some common themes contributing to successful implementation.

Partnership. The magnitude of change required for implementing an effective information literacy program requires the active partnership of faculty, librarians, administrators, students, presidents, and trustees. There needs to be a campuswide understanding and commitment if a campus culture is to change.

Experimentation. The design of an effective information literacy program, complemented by a resource-based learning strategy, requires experimentation. We must be willing to experiment and to learn from our successes as well as our failures. This experimentation needs to take place in a collegial supportive environment. The important thing is a move to action in order to better understand what strategies for implementing information literacy programs work best for students on a specific campus.

Integration. Traditional library orientation and bibliographic instruction programs have failed to command the interest of students and to satisfy the expectations of faculty. Effective information literacy programs must be embedded in specific courses and progress developmentally throughout an entire curriculum. The importance of information literacy for today's graduates argues against such instruction being pedantic or random.

Active Learning. Information literacy, like any other skill, must be practiced in order to be learned. Students who have grown comfortable with passive modes of instruction need to accept the challenge to become involved in their own learning. The strategy of resource-based learning is the most effective way to implement this change. In an information-rich environment, students need to develop the ability to locate, evaluate, synthesize, organize, and apply information.

Independent Learning. The expertly processed and predigested information presented in lectures and textbooks is the antithesis of resource-based learning. The former develops students as dependent learners, whereas the latter encourages students to become independent learners. Independent learning builds self-confidence and self-esteem and prepares a student to meet newly emerging expectations of employers in the Information Age.

The Challenge

Higher education has traditionally responded to the changing needs of society. If colleges and universities fail to meet the challenge of preparing students for the new Information Age, other postsecondary institutions will be invented to meet the need. The irony is that information literacy simply puts to the test the traditional rhetoric of higher education that colleges and universities are preparing students to know how to learn. New information technologies applied to an information-rich environment require that students learn new ways to access, evaluate, select, and apply information. Effective information literacy and resource-based learning programs provide a demonstrable way for students to show that they have developed what faculty have always insisted is a fundamental skill: the ability to reason one's way to valid conclusions utilizing the best information resources available.

D. W. Farmer
Terrence F. Mech
Editors

Reference

Farmer, D. W. "Strategies for Change." In D. W. Steeples (ed.), *Managing Change in Higher Education*. New Directions for Higher Education, no. 71. San Francisco: Jossey-Bass, 1990.

D. W. FARMER is vice president for academic affairs at King's College, Wilkes-Barre, Pennsylvania.

TERRENCE F. MECH is director of the library at King's College.

Index

Accountability, 28. *See also* Assessment; Evaluation; Success
Accreditation, and information literacy and resource-based learning, 18, 21-23, 24-25
Ackerson, L., 70, 71
Action Community on Information Literacy, 9
Administrators, and program development, 20
Alberta, University of, 37, 40, 42
Allen, J. P., 58, 61
Ambrose, H. W., III., 47, 48, 52
Ambrose, K. P., 47, 48, 52
American Association for Higher Education (AAHE), 9
American Association of Colleges for Teacher Education, 8
American Association of School Administrators, 8
American Library Association: Association of College and Research Libraries, 19, 25; and Cornell information literacy program, 99; Presidential Committee on Information Literacy, 8, 12, 103, 112
American Newspaper Publishers Association, 9
Architectural Alliance of Minnesota, framework for future library by, 32-34
Arizona State University, 74, 75, 77
Aronowitz, S., 113, 115, 121
Assessment: and integrated learning at King's College, 69-70; and resource-based learning, 119-120. *See also* Accountability; Evaluation; Success
Association for Supervision and Curriculum Development, 9-10, 13, 61
Association of American Colleges, 115, 121
Astin, A., 28
Australia, 11

Banks, J., 59, 61
Barnes, S., 98, 100, 101
Bellah, R., 114, 115, 116, 121
Berger, K., 77, 81
Bibliographic instruction, 15, 16-17

Biology, resource-based learning projects in, 46-52
Birnbaum, R., 116, 121
Blake, V. P., 93, 101
Blystone, R. V., 45, 52
Bodi, S., 45, 52
Bowling Green University, 11
Boyer, E. L., 7, 13
Bradigan, P., 77, 81
Breivik, P. S., 2, 5, 8, 9, 13, 37, 43, 45, 52
Brennan, T. M., 45, 52
Brewer, C., 59, 61
Brigham Young University, 74, 75-76, 77, 78-81
Brightman, H., 118, 122
British Library, 11
Brottman, M., 76, 81
Brundage, C. A., 45, 52
Bush Foundation, 34
Butler, H. J., 77, 81

California Newsreel, 59, 61
Cheung, K.-K., 58, 62
China, 11
Chisholm, M., 8
Coalition for Cultural Pluralism, 56, 62
Cochran, L., 116, 122
Coleman, P., 45, 52
Colleges, information literacy at small, 73-74
Colorado, University of, 7
Columbia University School of Library Service, 7
Commission on Higher Education. *See* Middle States Commission on Higher Education
Commission on Institutions of Higher Education, 16, 25
Compaine, B. M., 94, 101
Computers: and Information Age, 6; workplace knowledge of, 101. *See also* Microcomputers; Technology
Coons, B., 98, 100, 101
Coordinated Collection, 32, 33
Cornell University, 64; information literacy at, 74; Mann Library information literacy instruction at, 94-101

Council of Biology Editors Style Manual Committee, 47, 52
Council of Chief State School Officers, 8, 9
Cross, K. P., 113, 122
Cultural pluralism, 56; and resource-based learning and information literacy, 56-57; at Seattle Central Community College, 57-61

deFur, P. L., 45, 52
Dornbusch, R., 27

Earlham College, information literacy at, 73-74, 81
Education: information literacy, 93-101; transforming, through resource-based learning, 113-121
Education Commission of the States, 8
Electronic library, 91-92; and literacy, 92-93
Emory and Henry College, 64
England, 11-12
Evaluating the Library (Commission on Higher Education), 16
Evaluation: and information literacy programs, 23-24; at Seattle Central Community College, 58. *See also* Accountability; Assessment; Success

Faculty: barriers to information literacy for, 104-107; in framework for future library, 34; and integrated learning at King's College, 68; and program development, 19-20; and resource-based assignments, 50-52; role of, with information literacy, 40-41; and transformation of education, 115-119
Farber, E., 74, 81
Farmer, D. W., 2, 3, 103, 112, 123, 125
Fink, D., 59, 62
Fisher, V., 10
Framework for Outcomes Assessment (Commission on Higher Education), 17, 22
Freire, P., 116, 117, 122
French, N., 77, 81

Gardner, J. N., 42, 43
Gateway, 77-78
Gaunt, M. I., 2, 83, 90
Gee, E. G., 3n, 7, 37, 43, 45, 52

Geertz, C., 113, 122
Gelfand, M. A., 16, 25
Georgia State University, 118
Giroux, H., 113, 115, 116, 119, 121, 122
Gratch, B., 56, 62
Gutierrez, C., 70, 71

Harman, D., 92, 101
Henry, M., 119, 122
Hill, P. J., 59, 62
Hispanic Policy Development Project, 9
Hodgkinson, H., 28
Hotchkiss, S. K., 45, 52
Howard, J., 70, 71
Hunter, C., 92, 101

IBM Rochester, 29
Illinois, University of, at Urbana, 74, 75, 76, 77
Information, in Information Age, 6-7
Information Age: education for, 5-7; literacy in, 1-2
Information Industry Association, 9
Information literacy, 1-3, 8, 11, 55-56, 123-125; Association of Supervision and Curriculum Development resolution on, 9-10; barriers to, 103-112; and cultural pluralism, 56-57; faculty role with, 40-41; and instructional development, 38-40; international, 11-12; at King's College, 63-71; and Middle States Association Commission on Higher Education, 15-25; in Minnesota State University System, 31-32; at Rutgers University, 83-90; at small colleges, 73-74; and student services, 41-42; at universities, 74-81. *See also* Resource-based learning
Information literacy education, 93-94, at Cornell's Mann Library, 94-101
Information Literacy: Revolution in the Library (Breivik and Gee), 37, 38, 39, 41, 43
Instructional development, and information literacy, 38-40

Jacobson, F., 65, 71
Jakobovits, L. A., 45, 52
Johnstone, R., 73-74
Jones, L. B., 2, 27, 35

Katz, J., 119, 122
King's College, information literacy program at, 63-71

Kohl, D., 69, 71
Kotler, P., 119, 122
Kroll, S., 77, 81

Levine, A., 5, 13
Librarians: barriers to information literacy for, 107-109; and information literacy at universities, 75; and integrated learning at King's College, 68-69
Library(ies): and academic excellence, 7-8; electronic, 91-93; future academic, 30-31; framework for future, 32-34; time spent in, 7
Literacy, and electronic library, 92-93. See also Information literacy
Lizotte, R. S., 46, 52
Loe, M., 76, 81
Loughborough University, 12

MacAdam, B., 77, 81
MacDonald, B., 93, 101
MacGregor, J., 57, 62
McHenry, K. E., 2, 11, 55, 62
Malcolm Baldrige Award, 29
Maloney, Y., 45, 52
Mann Library, Cornell's, information literacy at, 94-101
Maryland, University of, at College Park, 78
Mech, T. F., 3, 125
Meier, M. S., 58, 62
Mensching, G. E., 59, 62
Mensching, T. B., 59, 62
Meyer, H. E., 6, 13
Michigan, University of, 74, 75, 77
Microcomputers, and information literacy, 42. See also Computers; Technology
Middle States Commission on Higher Education (CHE), 10, 15-16; accreditation emphasis of, 18; accreditation process of, 21-23; history of information literacy and, 16-18; on responsibility for developing programs, 19-21; on self-study and evaluation process, 23-24; suggestions from, 24-25
Minnesota Interlibrary Telecommunications Exchange (MINITEX) Library Information Network, 33
Minnesota Quality Council, 29
Minnesota State University System, 2, 27, 28, 29, 32, 33, 35; framework for future library for, 32-34; future library for, 30-31; on information literacy, 31-32; on measuring success, 28-29; on observing progress, 29; Q-7 Initiative of, 30; report of, 34-35
Minnich, E. K., 114, 122
Moran, B. B., 45, 52
Morganti, D., 65, 71
Murphy, P., 119, 122

Nahl-Jakobovits, D., 45, 52
Nash, S., 2, 83, 90
National Association of Counties, 9
National Board of Employment, Education, and Training, 11, 13
National Education Association, 9
National Forum for Black Public Administrators, 9
National Forum on Information Literacy, 9, 10
National Institute of Education, 115, 117, 119, 122
Nellis, M. K., 45, 52
Nelsen, W. C., 119, 122
New York, State University of, at Buffalo, 74, 77
Northwestern University, 74

Ochs, M., 98, 100, 101
Ohio State University, 74, 75, 76, 77-78
Olsen, J. K., 2, 91, 95, 102

Pence, J. L., 2, 113, 116, 122
Penhale, S. J., 45, 52
Pennsylvania State University, 65
Peters, T., 117, 122
Philadelphia College of Pharmacy and Science: freshman projects at, 46-47; resource learning at, 45-46, 50-52; senior projects at, 47-50
Ploski, H. A., 58, 62
Porter, J. R., 2, 45, 53
Presidents, and program development, 20-21
Prince Edward Island, University of, 42
Project for Automated Library Systems, 33
Purpel, D., 115, 122

Rader, H., 11
Resource-based learning, 1, 9, 55, 123-

Resource-based learning *(continued)* 125; beneficiaries of, 12; international, 11-12; leadership organizations for, 9-10; and Middle States Association, 15-25; paradigms for, 10-11; Philadelphia College of Pharmacy and Science projects for, 45-52; at Seattle Central Community College, 55-61; and transforming education, 113-121. *See also* Information literacy

Rivera, F., 58, 62
Rovner, S. J., 46, 52
Rutgers University, information literacy pilot project at, 83-90

Samford University, 11
Santa Fe Community College, 117
Santayana, G., 68
School Match, 8
Seattle Central Community College, 11; resource-based learning at, 57-61
Segal, J., 77, 81
Seldin, P., 115, 117, 119, 122
Self-studies, and information literacy programs, 23-24
Selin, H., 45, 52
Shirley, R., 119, 122
Simmons, H. L., 2, 10, 15, 23, 25
Sims, S., 77, 81
Spragg, E., 95, 101
Stachacz, J. C., 45, 52
Stanford, L. M., 2, 37, 43
Stewart, J. T., 2, 11, 55, 62
Stewart, L., 95, 102
Stockton State College, 70
Student services, and information literacy, 41-42
Students: barriers to information literacy for, 109-111; as independent learners, 123; and program development, 20; and resource-based assignments, 50-52
Study guides, at King's College, 64
Style, E., 59
Success, Minnesota measurement of, 28-29. *See also* Accountability; Assessment; Evaluation
Svinicki, M. D., 118, 122

Taylor, N., 45, 52
Teaching, cultural pluralism, 56-57. *See also* Faculty
Technology: and academic library of future, 31; information literacy, 111; for information literacy instruction, 76-78; and integrated learning at King's College, 69. *See also* Computers; Microcomputers
Texas, University of, at Austin, 64
Tiefel, V., 78, 81
Tierney, J., 2, 63, 71
Tjoumas, R., 93, 101
Towson State University, 10
Train, M. A., 70, 71
Trustees, and program development, 20-21
Turner, E. J., 58, 61

U.S. National Commission on Excellence in Education, 94, 102
Universities, information literacy at, 74-81
Upcraft, M. L., 42, 43

Van Cleve, J. V., 58, 62
Van Ostrand, D., 98, 100, 101
Victoria, University of, 42

Ware, S., 65, 71
Washington, University of, 74, 75, 76, 77
Wedgeworth, R., 8, 13
Weimer, M., 117, 122
Western State College of Colorado, 65
Wiggins, M. E., 2, 73, 81
Williams, J., 58, 62
Wilson, L., 69, 71
Workstation, 91
Writing, Rutgers University pilot project on, 83-90
Wu, J. L., 2, 11, 55, 62

Yogi, S., 58, 62
Young, V., 70, 71

ZYTEC, 29

Ordering Information

NEW DIRECTIONS FOR HIGHER EDUCATION is a series of paperback books that provides timely information and authoritative advice about major issues and administrative problems confronting every institution. Books in the series are published quarterly in Fall, Winter, Spring, and Summer and are available for purchase by subscription as well as by single copy.

SUBSCRIPTIONS for 1992 cost $45.00 for individuals (a savings of 20 percent over single-copy prices) and $60.00 for institutions, agencies, and libraries. Please do not send institutional checks for personal subscriptions. Standing orders are accepted.

SINGLE COPIES cost $14.95 when payment accompanies order. (California, New Jersey, New York, and Washington, D.C., residents please include appropriate sales tax.) Billed orders will be charged postage and handling.

DISCOUNTS FOR QUANTITY ORDERS are available. Please write to the address below for information.

ALL ORDERS must include either the name of an individual or an official purchase order number. Please submit your order as follows:
 Subscriptions: specify series and year subscription is to begin
 Single copies: include individual title code (such as HE1)

MAIL ALL ORDERS TO:
 Jossey-Bass Publishers
 350 Sansome Street
 San Francisco, California 94104

FOR SALES OUTSIDE OF THE UNITED STATES CONTACT:
 Maxwell Macmillan International Publishing Group
 866 Third Avenue
 New York, New York 10022

OTHER TITLES AVAILABLE IN THE
NEW DIRECTIONS FOR HIGHER EDUCATION SERIES
Martin Kramer, Editor-in-Chief

HE77 The Campus and Environmental Responsibility, *David W. Orr, David J. Eagan*
HE76 Administration as a Profession, *Jonathan D. Fife, Lester F. Goodchild*
HE75 Faculty in Governance: The Role of Senates and Joint Committees in Academic Decision Making, *Robert Birnbaum*
HE74 The Changing Dimensions of Student Aid, *Jamie P. Merisotis*
HE73 Using Consultants Successfully, *Jon F. Wergin*
HE72 Administrative Careers and the Marketplace, *Kathryn M. Moore, Susan B. Twombly*
HE71 Managing Change in Higher Education, *Douglas W. Steeples*
HE70 An Agenda for the New Decade, *Larry W. Jones, Franz Nowotny*
HE69 Financial Planning Under Economic Uncertainty, *Richard E. Anderson, Joel W. Meyerson*
HE67 Achieving Assessment Goals Using Evaluation Techniques, *Peter J. Gray*
HE66 Improving Undergraduate Education in Large Universities, *Carol H. Pazandak*
HE65 The End of Mandatory Retirement: Effects on Higher Education, *Karen C. Holden, W. Lee Hansen*
HE64 Successful Strategic Planning: Case Studies, *Douglas W. Steeples*
HE63 Research Administration and Technology Transfer, *James T. Kenny*
HE62 Making Computers Work for Administrators, *Kenneth C. Green, Steven W. Gilbert*
HE61 Leaders on Leadership: The College Presidency, *James L. Fisher, Martha W. Tack*
HE60 Increasing Retention: Academic and Student Affairs Administrators in Partnership, *Martha McGinty Stodt, William M. Klepper*
HE59 Student Outcomes Assessment: What Institutions Stand to Gain, *Diane F. Halpern*
HE58 Financing Higher Education: Strategies After Tax Reform, *Richard E. Anderson, Joel W. Meyerson*
HE57 Creating Career Programs in a Liberal Arts Context, *Mary Ann F. Rehnke*
HE56 Managing Programs for Learning Outside the Classroom, *Patricia Senn Breivik*
HE53 Managing College Enrollments, *Don Hossler*
HE52 Making the Budget Process Work, *David J. Berg, Gerald M. Skogley*
HE51 Incentive for Faculty Vitality, *Roger G. Baldwin*
HE45 Women in Higher Education Administration, *Adrian Tinsley, Cynthia Secor, Sheila Kaplan*